What Is Liberalism?

Englished and Adapted

From the Spanish of Dr. Don Felix Sarda Y Salvany

by: Conde B. Pallen, Ph.D., LL.D.

Table of Contents

Preface

In 1886 there appeared in Spain a little work under the title El Liberalismo es Pecado, "Liberalism Is a Sin," by Don Felix Sarda y Salvany, a priest of Barcelona and editor of a journal called La Revista Popular. The book excited considerable commotion. It was vigorously assailed by the Liberals. A Spanish Bishop of a Liberal turn instigated an answer to Dr. Sarda's work by way of another Spanish priest. Both books were sent to Rome, praying the Sacred Congregation of the Index to put Dr. Sarda's work under the ban. The following letter, under date of January 10, 1887, from the Sacred Congregation itself, explains the result of its consideration of the two volumes:

Most Excellent Sir:

The Sacred Congregation of the Index has received the denunciation of the little work bearing the title El Liberalismo es Pecado by Don Felix Sarda y Salvany, a priest of your diocese; the denunciation was accompanied at the same time by another little work, entitled El Proceso del Integrismo, that is, "A refutation of the errors contained in the little work El Liberalismo es Pecado." The author of the second work is D. de Pazos, a canon of the diocese of Vich.

Whereupon, the Sacred Congregation has carefully examined both works and decided as follows: In the first, not only is nothing found contrary to sound doctrine, but its author, D. Felix Sarda, merits great praise for his exposition and defense of the sound doctrine therein set forth with solidity, order and lucidity, and without personal offense to anyone.

The same judgment, however, cannot be passed on the other work, that by D. de Pazos, for in matter it needs corrections. Moreover, his injurious manner of speaking cannot be approved, for he inveighs rather against the person of D. Sarda than against the latter's supposed errors.

Therefore, the Sacred Congregation has commanded D. de Pazos, admonished by his own Bishop, to withdraw his book, as far as he can, from circulation, and in the future, if any discussion of the subject should arise, to abstain from all expressions personally injurious, according to the precept of true Christian charity; and this all the more since Our Holy Father, Leo XIII, whereas he urgently recommends castigation of error, neither desires nor approves expressions personally injurious, especially when directed against those who are eminent for their doctrine and their piety.

In communicating to you this order of the Sacred Congregation of the Index, that you may be able to make it known to the illustrious priest of your diocese, D. Sarda, for his peace of mind, I pray God to grant you all happiness and prosperity, and subscribe myself with great respect,

Your most obedient servant,
FR. JEROME SECHERI, O.P.
Secretary of the Sacred Congregation Of the Index.

To The Most Rev. Jacobo Catala et Alboso, Bishop of Barcelona.

The following short chapters on Liberalism are mainly and substantially Dr. Sarda's book, put into English, and adapted to our American conditions. Their need and their use will be best understood and appreciated by their perusal.

What Begets Liberalism

Physical science tells us that floating through the atmosphere are innumerable disease germs seeking a suitable nidus in which to settle and propagate and that we are constantly breathing these germs into the lungs. If the system be depleted or weakened, the dangerous microbe takes up its abode with us, and propagating its own kind with astonishing rapidity, undermines and ravages our health. The only safeguard against the encroachments of this insidious enemy, which we cannot escape, is a vigorous and healthy body with adequate powers of resistance to repel the invader.

It is equally true that we are subject to like infectious attacks in the spiritual order. Swarming in the atmosphere of our spiritual lives are innumerable deadly germs, ever ready to fasten upon the depleted and weakened soul and, propagating its leprous contagion through every faculty, destroy the spiritual life. Against the menace of this ever-threatening danger, whose advances we cannot avoid in our present circumstances, the ever-healthy soul alone can be prepared. To escape the contagion, the power of resistance must be equal to the emergencies of the attack, and that power will be in proportion to our spiritual health. To be prepared is to be armed, but to be prepared is not sufficient; we must possess the interior strength to throw off the germ. There must be no condition in the soul to make a suitable nidus for an enemy so insidious and so efficacious as to need only the slightest point of contact whence to spread its deadly contagion.

It is not only through the avenues of disordered passions that this spiritual disease may gain an entrance; it may make its inroad through the intellect, and this under a disguise often calculated to deceive the unwary and incautious. The Trojans admitted the enemy into their walls under the impression that they were actually securing a valuable acquisition to their safety, and today their fatal experience has come down to us in the proverb--"Beware of the Greeks when they bring gifts." Intellectual torpidity, inexperience, ignorance, indifference, and complaisance, or even virtues, such as, benevolence, generosity, and pity may be the unsuspected way open to the foe, and lo, we are surprised to find him in possession of the citadel!

That we may know our danger, we must appreciate the possible shapes in which it may come. Here is just the difficulty; the uniform of the enemy is so various, changeable, sometimes even of our own colors, that if we rely upon the outward semblance alone, we shall be more often deceived than certain of his identity. But before laying down any test by which we may distinguish friend from foe in a warfare so subtly fought within the precincts of our own souls, let us first reconnoiter the respective positions of either camp, and to do this best, we shall consider the origin and sources of the danger which surrounds us, for we may be asked: "Where is this foe described as so intangible as scarcely to be apprehended by ordinary mortals?" Or it may be urged: "Is the danger as proximate, as frequent and [as] fearful as you allege? Whence is it anyhow? Point it out! If we know from what direction the enemy comes, we may better appreciate the peril."

As we are addressing ourselves to those who live amidst the peculiar circumstances of our American life, and as the spiritual and moral conditions which obtain in this country make up the moral and spiritual atmosphere in which we have our being, it is in the relation of our surroundings to ourselves as well as of ourselves to our surroundings that we shall find the answer to our question. Let us then consider these surroundings in a general way for the moment. First, as to some patent facts: The population of this country is at present something over sixty-three millions. (census 1890) Of these, ten million are Catholics, and according to their claim, twenty-three million are Protestants, leaving a population of thirty-three million or more who do not profess any form become mere differences of private opinion, dependent upon nothing but the caprice or choice of the individual. Amongst the twenty million Protestants every shade and variety of belief in the Christian dispensation finds easy lodgment, from the belief in the Incarnation and Consubstantiation to the rejection of the Divinity of Christ altogether in the vacuous creed of Unitarianism. In this scale of heresy the adjustment of creed are loose and easy. Lack of any decisive authority renders any exact standard of belief impossible. A protestant may freely range from one end of the scale tot he other and still be considered orthodox according to Protestant estimates. A loose, indefinite belief in Christ, either as God redeeming the world or even as a great ethical teacher, not God Himself though sent by God, suffices to place the Protestant within the compass of his own standqard of orthodoxy. Any specific expression of dogma or of particular truths, bound up in the acceptance of Christianity, is not

6

required; or, if required by any one sect or denomination, can find no authoritative exaction, for the differences between the sects, in the last resort, become mere differences of private opinion, dependent on nothing by the caprice r choice of the individual.

Outside of these various bodies of loosely professed Christians stands a still larger mass of our population who are either absolutely indifferent to Christianity as a creed or positively reject it. In practice, the distinction is of little moment whether they hold themselves merely indifferent or positively hostile. In other words, we have here to reckon with a body, to all practical purposes, that is infidel. This mass comprises over half of our population, holding itself aloof from Christianity, and in some instances virulently antagonistic to it. In distinct religious opposition to this mass of infidelity and Protestantism, Catholics find themselves sharply and radically opposed. Heresy and infidelity are irreconcilable with Catholicity. "He that is not with me is against me" (Matt. 12:30) are the words of Our Lord Himself, for denial of Catholic truth is the radical and common element of both heresy and infidelity. The difference between them is merely a matter of degree. One denies less, the other more. Protestantism, with its sliding scale of creeds, is Simply an inclined plane into the abyss of positive unbelief. It is always virtual infidelity, its final outcome open infidelity, as the thirty-three million unbelievers in this country stand witness.

We live in the midst of this religious anarchy. Fifrty-three millions of our population can, in one sense or other, be considered anti-Catholic. From this mass--heretical and infidel--exhales an atmosphere filled with germs poisonous and fatal to Catholic life, if permitted to take root in the Catholic heart. The mere force of gravitation, which the larger mass ever exercises upon the smaller, is a power which the most energetic vigor alone can resist. Under this dangerous influence, a deadly inertia is apt to creep over the souls of the incautious and is only to be overcome by the liveliest exercise of Catholic faith. To live without enervation amidst an heretical and infidel population requires a robust religious constitution. And to this danger we are daily exposed, ever coming into contact in a thousand ways, in almost every relation of life, with anti-Catholic thought and customs. But outside of this spiritual inertia, our non-Catholic surroundings--a danger rather passive than active in its influence--beget a still greater menace.

It is natural that Protestantism and infidelity should find public expression. What our sixty million non-Catholic population think in these matters naturally seeks and finds open expression. They have their organs and their literature where we find their current opinions publicly uttered. Their views upon reli gion, morality, politics, the constitution of society are perpetually marshaled before us. In the pulpit and in the press they are reiterated day after day. In magazine and newspaper they constantly speak from every line. Our literature is permeated and saturated with non-Catholic dogmatism. On all sides do we find this opposing spirit. We cannot escape from it. It enfolds and embraces us. Its breath is perpetually in our faces. It enters in by eye and ear. From birth to death, it enslaves us in its offensive garments. It now soothes and flatters, now hates and curses, now threatens, now praises. But it is most dangerous when it comes to us under the form of "liberality." It is especially powerful for seduction in this guise. And it is under this aspect that we wish to consider it. For it is as Liberalism that Protestantism and Infidelity make their most devastating inroads upon the domain of the Faith.

Out of these non-Catholic and anti-Catholic conditions thus predominating amongst us springs this monster of our times, Liberalism!

What Is Liberalism?

Protestantism naturally begets toleration of error. Rejecting the principle of authority in religion, it has neither criterion nor definition of faith. On the principle that every individual or sect may interpret the deposit of Revelation according to the dictates of private judgment, it gives birth to endless differences and contradictions. Impelled by the law of its own impotence, through lack of any decisive voice of authority in matters of faith, it is forced to recognize as valid and orthodox any belief that springs from the exercise of private judgment. Therefore does it finally arrive, by force of its own premises, at the conclusion that one creed is as good as another; it then seeks to shelter its inconsistency under the false plea of liberty of conscience. Belief is not imposed by a legitimately and divinely constituted authority, but springs directly and freely from the unrestricted exercise of the individual's reason or caprice upon the subject matter of Revelation. The individual or sect interprets as it pleases--rejecting or accepting what it chooses. This is popularly called liberty of conscience. Accepting this principle, Infidelity, on the same plea, rejects all Revelation, and Protestantism, which handed over the premise, is powerless to protest against the conclusion; for it is clear that one who, under the plea of rational liberty, has the right to repudiate any part of Revelation that may displease him, cannot logically quarrel with one who, on the same ground, repudiates the whole. If one creed is as good as another, on the plea of rational liberty, on the same plea, no creed is as good as any. Taking the field with this fatal weapon of Rationalism, Infidelity has stormed and taken the very citadel of Protestantism, helpless against the foe of its own making.

We find as a result amongst the people of this country (excepting well formed Catholics, of course) that authoritative and positive religion has met with utter disaster and that religious beliefs or unbeliefs have come to be mere matters of opinion, wherein there are always essential differences, each one being free to make or unmake his own creed--or accept no creed.

Such is the mainspring of the heresy constantly dinned into our ears, flooding our current literature and our press. It is against this that we have to be perpetually vigilant, the more so because it insidiously attacks us on the grounds of a false charity and in the name of a false liberty. Nor does it appeal to us only on the ground of religious toleration.

The principle ramifies in many directions, striking root into our domestic, civil, and political life, whose vigor and health depend upon the nourishing and sustaining power of religion. For religion is the bond which unites us to God, the Source and End of all good; and Infidelity, whether virtual, as in Protestantism, or explicit, as in Agnosticism, severs the bond which binds men to God and seeks to build human society on the foundations of man's absolute independence. Hence we find Liberalism laying down as the basis of its propaganda the following principles:

1. The absolute sovereignty of the individual in his entire independence of God and God's authority.

2. The absolute sovereignty of society in its entire independence of everything which does not proceed from itself.

3. Absolute civil sovereignty in the implied right of the people to make their own laws in entire independence and utter disregard of any other criterion than the popular will expressed at the polls and in parliamentary majorities.

4. Absolute freedom of thought in politics, morals, or in religion. The unrestrained liberty of the press.

Such are the radical principles of Liberalism. In the assumption of the absolute sovereignty of the individual, that is, his entire independence of God, we find the common source of all the others. To express them all in one term, they are, in the order of ideas, RATIONALISM, or the doctrine of the absolute sovereignty of human reason. Here human reason is made the measure and sum of truth. Hence we have individual, social, and political Rationalism, the corrupt fountainhead of liberalist principles [which are]: absolute freedom of worship, the supremacy of the State, secular education repudiating any connection with religion, marriage sanctioned and legitimatized by the State alone, etc.; in one word, which synthesizes all, we have Secularization, which denies religion any active intervention in the concerns of public and of private life, whatever they be. This is veritable social atheism.

Such is the source of liberalism in the order of ideas; such, in consequence of our Protestant and infidel surroundings, is the intellectual atmosphere which we are perpetually breathing into our souls. Nor do these principles remain simply in the speculative order, poised forever in the region of thought. Men are not mere contemplatives. Doctrines and beliefs inevitably precipitate themselves into action. The speculation of today becomes the deed of tomorrow, for men, by force of the law of their nature, are ever acting out what they think. Rationalism, therefore, takes concrete shape in the order of facts. It finds palpable expression and action in the press, in legislation, and in social life. The secular press reeks with it, proclaiming with almost unanimous vociferation, absolute division between public life and religion. It has become the shibboleth of journalism, and the editor who will not recognize it in his daily screed soon feels the dagger of popular disapproval. In secularized marriage and in our divorce laws, it cleaves the very roots of domestic society; in secularized education, the cardinal principle of our public school system, it propagates itself in the hearts of the future citizens and the future parents; in compulsory school laws, it forces in the entering wedge of socialism; in the speech and intercourse of social life, it is constantly asserting itself with growing reiteration; in secret societies, organized in a spirit destructive of religion and often for the express purpose of exterminating Catholicity, it menaces our institutions and places the country in the hands of conspirators, whose methods and designs, beyond the reach of the public eye, constitute a tyranny of darkness. In a thousand ways does the principle of Rationalism find its action and expression in social and civil life, and however diversified be its manifestation, there is in it always a unity and a system of opposition to Catholicity. Whether concerted or not, it ever acts in the same direction, and whatever special school within the genus of Liberalism professes it or puts it into action--be it in society, in domestic life, or in politics--the same essential characteristics will be found in all its protean shapes-- opposition to the Church--and it will ever be found stigmatizing the most ardent defenders of the Faith as reactionaries, clericals, Ultramontanes, etc.

Wherever found, whatever its uniform, Liberalism in its practical action is ever a systematic warfare upon the Church. Whether it intrigue, whether it legislate, whether it orate or assassinate, whether it call itself Liberty or Government or the State or Humanity or Reason, or whatnot, its fundamental characteristic is an uncompromising opposition to the Church.

Liberalism is a world complete in itself; it has its maxims, its fashions, its art, its literature, its diplomacy, its laws, its conspiracies, its ambuscades. It is the world of Lucifer, disguised in our times under the name of Liberalism, in radical opposition and in perpetual warfare against that society composed of the Children of God, the Church of Jesus Christ.

Liberalism Is A Sin

Liberalism, whether in the doctrinal or practical order, is a sin. In the doctrinal order, it is heresy, and consequently a mortal sin against faith. In the practical order, it is a sin against the commandments of God and of the Church, for it virtually transgresses all commandments. To be more precise: in the doctrinal order, Liberalism strikes at the very foundations of faith; it is heresy radical and universal, because within it are comprehended all heresies. In the practical order it is a radical and universal infraction of the divine law, since it sanctions and authorizes all infractions of that law.

Liberalism is a heresy in the doctrinal order because heresy is the formal and obstinate denial of all Christian dogmas in general. It repudiates dogma altogether and substitutes opinion, whether that opinion be doctrinal or the negation of doctrine. Consequently, it denies every doctrine in particular. If we were to examine in detail all the doctrines or dogmas which, within the range of Liberalism, have been denied, we would find every Christian dogma in one way or another rejected--from the dogma of the Incarnation to that of Infallibility.

None the less Liberalism is in itself dogmatic; and it is in the declaration of its own fundamental dogma, the absolute independence of the individual and the social reason, that it denies all Christian dogmas in general. Catholic dogma is the authoritative declaration of revealed truth--or a truth consequent upon Revelation--by its infallibly constituted exponent [the Pope]. This logically implies the obedient acceptance of the dogma on the part of the individual and of society. Liberalism refuses to acknowledge this rational obedience and denies the authority. It asserts the sovereignty of the individual and social reason and enthrones Rationalism in the seat of authority. It knows no dogma except the dogma of self-assertion. Hence it is heresy, fundamental and radical, the rebellion of the human intellect against God.

It follows, therefore, that Liberalism denies the absolute jurisdiction of Jesus Christ, who is God, over individuals and over society, and by consequence, repudiates the jurisdiction which God has delegated to the visible head of the Church over each and all of the faithful, whatever their condition or rank in life. Moreover, it denies the necessity of divine Revelation and the obligation of everyone to accept that Revelation under pain of eternal perdition. It denies the formal motive of faith, viz., the authority of God revealing, and admits only as much of revealed doctrine as it chooses or comprehends within its own narrow capacity. It denies the infallible magistracy of the Church and of the Pope, and consequently all the doctrines defined and taught by this divine authority. In short, it sets itself up as the measure and rule of faith and thus really shuts out Revelation altogether. It denies everything which it itself does not proclaim. It negates everything which it itself does not affirm. But not being able to affirm any truth beyond its own reach, it denies the possibility of any truth which it does not comprehend. The revelation of truth above human reason it therefore debars at the outset. The divinity of Jesus Christ is beyond its horoscope. The Church is outside its comprehension. The submission of human reason to the Word of Christ or its divinely constituted exponent is to it intolerable. It is, therefore, the radical and universal denial of all divine truth and Christian dogma, the primal type of all heresy, and the supreme rebellion against the authority of God and His Church. As with Lucifer, its maxim is, "I will not serve."

Such is the general negation uttered by Liberalism. From this radical denial of revealed truth in general naturally follows the denial of particular dogmas, in whole or in part (as circumstances present them in opposition to its rationalistic judgment). Thus, for instance, it denies the validity of faith by Baptism, when it admits or supposes the equality of any or all reli gious cults; it denies the sanctity of marriage when it sanctions so-called civil marriages; it denies the infallibility of the Roman Pontiff, when it refuses to accept as laws his official commands and teachings and subjects them to the scrutiny of its own intellect--not to assure itself of their authenticity, as is legitimate, but to sit in defiant judgment upon their contents.

When we come to the practical order, Liberalism is radical immorality. Morality requires a standard and a guide for rational action; it postulates a hierarchy of ends, and therefore of order, within whose series there is a subordination of means to the attainment of an ultimate purpose. It therefore requires a principle or fundamental rule of all action, by which the subject of moral acts, the rational creature, determines his course and guides himself to the attainment of his end. In the moral order, the Eternal Reason alone can be that principle or fundamental rule of action, and this Eternal Reason is God. In the moral order, the created reason, with power to determine its course, must guide itself by the light of the Uncreated Reason, Who is the beginning and end of all things. The law, therefore, imposed by the Eternal Reason upon the creature must be the principle or rule of morality. Hence, obedience and submission in the moral order is an absolute requisite of morality. But Liberalism has proclaimed the absurd principle of the absolute sovereignty of human reason; it denies any reason beyond itself and asserts its independence in the order of knowledge, and hence in the order of action or morality. Here we have morality without law, without order, freedom to do what one pleases, or what comes to the same thing, morality which is not morality, for morality implies the idea not only of direction, but also essentially demands that of restraint and limitation under the control of law. Liberalism in the order of action is license, recognizing no principle or rule beyond itself.

We may then say of Liberalism: in the order of ideas it is absolute error; in the order of facts it is absolute disorder. It is, therefore, in both cases a very grievous and deadly sin, for sin is rebellion against God in thought or in deed, the enthronement of the creature in the place of the Creator.

The Gravity Of The Sin Of Liberalism

Liberalism is a mortal sin. But Catholic theology teaches us that all sins are not equally grave, that there is even a distinction of degree in venial sins. There are also degrees in the category of mortal sin, just as there are in the category of meritorious works. The gravity of sin is determined by the object at which it strikes. Blasphemy, for instance, which directly attacks God Himself, is a sin of much graver character than theft, which directly attacks man. With the exception of formal hatred against God, which constitutes the deadliest of all sins and of which the creature is rarely culpable--unless he be in Hell--the gravest of all sins are those against faith. The reason is evident. Faith is the foundation of the supernatural order, and sin is sin insofar as it attacks this supernatural order at one or another point; hence that is the greatest sin which attacks this order at its very foundations. To destroy the foundations is to destroy the entire superstructure. To cut off the branch of a tree will not kill it, but to lay the axe to the trunk or to the roots is fatal to its life. Henceforth it bears neither blossom nor fruit. St. Augustine, cited by St. Thomas, characterizes sin against faith in these words: Hoc est peccatum quo tenentur cuncta peccata. "This is the sin which comprehends all other sins."

The Angel of the Schools expresses himself with his usual clearness on this point: "The gravity of sin is determined by the interval which it places between man and God; now sin against faith separates man from God as far as possible, since it deprives him of the true knowledge of God; it therefore follows that sin against faith is the greatest of all sins."

When sin against faith is simply a culpable privation of the knowledge of God, it has not the same gravity as a direct and formal attack upon dogmas expressly defined by divine Revelation. In this latter case, sin against faith, so grave in itself, acquires that degree of gravity which constitutes heresy. It then contains all the malice of infidelity and becomes an express protestation against the teachings of faith or an express adherence to a teaching which is condemned as false and erroneous by the Faith itself. Besides the deadly sin against faith itself, it is accompanied by hardness of heart, obstinacy, and the proud preference for one's own reason over the reason of God Himself.

Hence, heretical doctrines--and works inspired by them--constitute the greatest of all sins, with the exception of formal hatred against God, of which only the demons in Hell and the damned are capable. Liberalism, then, which is heresy, and all the works of Liberalism, which are heretical works, are the gravest sins known in the code of the Christian law.

Liberalism is, therefore, a greater sin than blasphemy, theft, adultery, homicide, or any other violation of the law of God, save in such case as where one acts in good faith, in ignorance, or without thought.

It is true that modern naturalism does not so regard or understand the case. But the law of the Church in matters of morals and doctrines is unchangeable; it ordains today as it did yesterday, and heresy is always heresy, no matter what the shape it takes. Appearances may be fair, and the devil may present himself as an angel of light. The danger is the greater as the outward show is more seductive. Heresy has never been so insidious as under its present form of Liberalism. Its range is so wide that it touches upon every note in the scale and finds an easy disguise in its protean facilities. But its most fatal shaft is in its plea for "liberality of mind." This, in its own eyes, is its cardinal virtue. "Intellectual freedom from dogmatism" is its boast, a boast in reality the mask of ignorance and pride. To meet such an enemy requires no ordinary courage, which must be guarded by a sleepless vigilance. When encountered, it is obligatory upon the Catholic conscience to resist it with all the powers of the soul. Heresy and all its works are sins; Liberalism is the root of heresy, the tree of evil in whose branches all the harpies of infidelity find ample shelter; it is today the evil of all evils.

The Degrees Of Liberalism

As a system of doctrines, Liberalism may be called a school; if we regard it as an organization of adepts for the purpose of spreading and propagating its doctrines, it may be called a sect; inasmuch as it is a group of men seeking the political enforcement of its doctrines, it may be called a party. But in whatever aspect we consider it--whether as a school or sect or party (it presents itself in various degrees or shades), yet it is still nonetheless Liberalism because variant, for with specific and logical unity there may be a multitudinous variety.

Now the unity of Liberalism is not positive but negative; it has no unity of its own; it is by virtue of its opposition to truth, which is essentially one, that Liberalism becomes accidentally one. As the vis-a-vis of truth, it possesses the unity of opposition: The different degrees of its denial will constitute the degrees of its opposition and so give us the varieties in the negative unity of its denial. Denial is its unity in general, and this ranges through the entire realm of negation, the degree of denial being determined by the degree of truth denied. If men were absolutely logical and followed to their ultimate conclusions the premises which they lay down, they would become angels or devils in working out the consequences according to the goodness or badness of their first principles. But men are not always logical; they often stop short of the consequences logically flowing from the premises preceding. We, therefore, as a rule, see the good as only half good and the bad as not altogether bad. Hence we find few out-and-out Liberals. Not many go the full length of their principles. They are nevertheless true Liberals, that is, veritable disciples, partisans or followers of Liberalism, ranging themselves under its banner, either as a school, a sect or a party.

There are Liberals who accept its principles but reject the consequences, at least those most repugnant or extreme. For instance, there are men who believe that the Catholic Church is the great enemy of modern progress, the one great object in the way of the triumph of their principles. Why not then openly persecute the Church and endeavor to wipe her off the face of the earth, as a Nero or a Domitian sought to do? No, they would not go to this extreme, although it is the practical consequence of their premise. Or again, if they shrink from the terrors of bloodshed and the horrors of assassination, why do they not close our Catholic schools, the nurseries of the Faith? To permit the existence of these schools is to allow the active and rapid propagation of the Faith. If Catholicity be the evil they affirm it to be, would they not be perfectly logical in nipping it in the bud, that is, in the schoolroom? But no, they would not go so far. Yet the suppression of the Catholic parochial school is the surest means to strangle the Faith in our midst. Why should there be any compunction in rooting out the greatest evil--in their estimation--which afflicts our age, the one great dyke against the flood of human "liberties" (now rising almost to the level of the opposing barrier)? It is because these Liberals are inconsistent; they shrink from the logic of conclusions.

Again, there are Liberals who accept such and such conclusions, or their application, but scrupulously repudiate the principles whence they flow. They believe, for instance, in absolutely secularizing education, and yet reject the doctrine of atheism, which is the only soil congenial to its growth. They applaud the result, while they repudiate the cause.

Some would apply Liberalism only to education; others only to the civil order; and others still, only to political life.

It is the most advanced alone who seek to apply it to everything and for everything. The attenuations and mutilations of the liberal Credo are as many as the interests advanced or balked at by its application. It is generally supposed that men think with their heads, but their intelligence often has less to do with it than their hearts--and not infrequently their stomachs determine their conclusions. Liberalism is thus often measured out by the dose, according to the taste of the consumer, as liquors are to drinkers, according to the appetite of each. This one, in comparison to his more advanced neighbor (who appears to him a brutal demagogue), is no Liberal at all; whereas, his less advanced neighbor is, in his eyes, an out-and-out reactionary, rooted in a stagnant past. It is simply a question of degree, whose grades slide variously along the liberal scale, some nearer some farther from the abyss. From the baptized or even surpliced Liberal, who boasts his breadth of mind in his easy toleration of error, to the avowed atheist, who hurls his open defiance against God, the difference is only one of degree. One simply stands on a higher rung of the same ladder than the other. Observe, when pushed to the wall, how all alike claim the same denomination of liberal. They may even regard each other with aversion, but all invoke the same appellation as finally descriptive of each. Their common criterion is "liberality" and "independence of mind"; the degree of application will be measured by the individual disposition, more or less depending upon the variety of elements in the makeup of the individual and his surroundings: self-interest with one, temperament with another, education with a third, impeding a too-rapid gait on the road to absolute Liberalism; human respect may moderate another, serving as a balance--weight to his rashness; family or school or business relations may clog the footsteps of a fourth. A thousand and one things may serve as a brake to a too-accelerated descent, not to mention that satanic prudence which counsels a conservative advance in order not to alarm the timid. This last fashion of procedure often serves as a mask to the most advanced Liberals, who hide their designs under the appearance of a frank demagoguery. Sometimes Liberalism stalks along in the careless trappings of an easy-going good nature or a simplicity of character, which invites our affection and allays our suspicion. Its very candor in this guise is an aggression difficult to resist. It does not appear responsible and excites our compassion before it has awakened our aversion. We seem to forgive it before we accuse it. But all the greater is the danger when it appears least possible.

Such are the various fashions of Liberalism. Its disguises are many, its degrees various. Withal, however, it is the same evil, though motley be its trappings. Liberalism is one; whereas Liberals, like bad wine, differ in color and taste.

Catholic Liberalism Or Liberal Catholicism

Peace in war is an incongruity. Foes in the midst of battle cannot well be friends. Where the pressure of conflicting forces is most intense, there is little opportunity of reconciliation. Yet this absurdity and contradiction we find in the odious and repulsive attempt to unite Liberalism with Catholicism. The monstrosity resulting is what is known as the Liberal Catholic or the Catholic Liberal. Strange as it may seem, Catholics with good intentions have paid tribute to this absurdity and indulged the vain hope of peace with the eternal enemy.

This fatal error has its source in the vain and exaggerated desire of reconciling and harmonizing in peace, doctrines utterly incompatible and hostile by their very nature.

Liberalism is the dogmatic affirmation of the absolute independence of the individual and of the social reason. Catholicity is the dogma of the absolute subjection of the individual and of the social order to the revealed law of God. One doctrine is the exact antithesis of the other. They are opposites in direct conflict. How is it possible to reconcile them? Opposition here necessarily means conflict, and the two can no more harmonize than the square can be made one with the circle.

To the promoters of Catholic Liberalism the thing appears easy enough. "It is admirable," they say, "for the individual reason to be subject to the law of God if it so wishes, but we must distinguish between the public and the private reason, especially in an age like ours. The modern State does not recognize God or the Church. In the conflict of different religious creeds, the public reason must stand neutral and impartial. Hence the necessary independence of the public reason. The State as State can have no reli gion. Let the simple citizen, if he wishes, submit to the revelation of Jesus Christ, but the statesman and the man in public life must comport himself as if no Revelation existed." Now all this means civil or social atheism. It means that society is independent of God, its Author; that while individuals may recognize their dependence on the divine law, civil society should not-- a distinction whose sophism is founded on an intolerable contradiction.

It is clear that, if the individual reason is obliged to submit to the law of God, the public and the social reason cannot logically escape the same duty without falling into an extravagant dualism by virtue of which men would be forced to submit to the law of two contrary and opposed consciences. Privately, men would have to be Christian; publicly they would be free to be atheistic. Furthermore, the road is open to an odious tyranny, for if the public conscience were independent of the Christian law and ignored it, there would be no public recognition of the obligation by the civil arm to protect the Church in the exercise of her rights. Nay, more, the civil power would readily become the means of persecution, and rulers hostile to the Church, condemning divine law, could actually, under cover of authority, legislate against Christianity. Nor is this a fanciful picture, for France and Italy, legislating today on the basis of the sovereign independence of the social and public reason, have enacted odious laws which hold the Church in those countries in distressful legal bondage. And the Holy Father himself is now a prisoner within the walls of the Vatican on account of the violent usurpation of his domains by an atheist government. But the results of the fatal distinction do not stop with the functions of legislation and administration subjecting the Church to social and civil persecution; in modern times it has gone further still and extends its baneful influence to the schoolroom, propagating itself by placing the education of youth under its dominating influence. It forms the conscience of youth, not according to the divine law, which acknowledges the will of God, but upon a premeditated and careful ignorance of that law. It is as secular education that it seizes upon the future and breeds atheism in the hearts of the coming generations.

The Catholic Liberalist or the Liberal Catholic, admitting this fatal distinction between the private and the public reason, thus throws open the gates to the enemies of the faith, and posing as a man of intellect with generous and liberal views, stultifies reason by his gross offense against the principle of contradiction. He is thus both a traitor and a fool. Seeking to please the enemies of the Faith, he has betrayed his trust, the Faith itself; imagining he is upholding the rights of reason, he surrenders it in the most abject way to the spirit of denial, the spirit of untruth. He has not the courage to withstand the derision of his cunning foe. To be called intolerant, illiberal, narrow, ultramontane, reactionist, is gall and wormwood to his little soul. Under this epithetical fire he gives way and surrenders his birthright of faith and reason for a mess of Liberal pottage.

Intrinsic Causes Of Liberal Catholicism

Strange as may seem that anomaly called Liberal Catholicism, its reason is not far to seek. It takes its root in a false conception of the nature of the act of faith. The Liberal Catholic assumes as the formal motive of the act of faith, not the infallible authority of God revealing supernatural truth, but his own reason deigning to accept as true what appears rational to him according to the appreciation and measure of his own individual judgment. He subjects God's authority to the scrutiny of his reason, and not his reason to God's authority. He accepts Revelation, not on account of the infallible Revealer, but because of the "infallible" receiver. With him the individual judgment is the rule of faith. He believes in the independence of reason. It is true he accepts the Magisterium of the Church, yet he does not accept it as the sole authorized expounder of divine truth. He reserves, as a coefficient factor in the determination of that truth, his own private judgment. The true sense of revealed doctrine to him is not always certain, and human reason therefore has something to say in the matter, as for instance, the limits of the Church's infallibility may be determined by human science. Within lines thus prescribed, the declarations of the Church to him are infallible, but these limits are not to be determined by the Church herself. Science will do that for her. She is of course infallible, they say, but we will determine when and in what she shall speak infallibly. Such is the absurdity which the Liberal Catholic falls into by placing the formal motive of faith in human reason.

The Liberal Catholic calls himself a Catholic because he firmly believes Catholicity to be the veritable revelation of the Son of God; he calls himself a Liberal Catholic because he believes that no one can impose upon him any belief which his individual judgment does not measure as perfectly rational. What is not rational he rejects; he is intellectually free to accept or reject. What appears good he assents to, but he is intellectually bound to no one. Thus, unwittingly, he falls an easy victim to the snare set by the devil for the intellectually proud. He has substituted the naturalistic principle of free examination for the supernatural principle of faith. As a consequence, he is really not Christian, but pagan. He has no real supernatural faith, but only a simple human conviction. In the acceptance of the principle that the individual reason is thus free to believe or not to believe, Liberal

Catholics are deluded into the notion that incredulity is a virtue rather than a vice. They fail to see in it an infirmity of the understanding, a voluntary blindness of the heart, and a consequent weakness of will. On the other hand, they look upon the skeptical attitude as a legitimate condition wherein intellectual freedom is preserved, the skeptic remaining master of himself to believe or deny. They have a horror of any coercive element in matters of faith; any chastisement of error shocks their tender susceptibilities, and they detest any Catholic legislation in the direction of what they are pleased to call intolerance. The Syllabus of Errors of Pius IX is a nightmare to them, a most inopportune, dominating, harsh, and peremptory document, calculated to offend the sensibilities of the Protestant and modern world; it need not be accepted as an infallible utterance, and, if accepted, must be taken in a very modified sense. The ultramontane interpretation to him is violent and extreme, and does much more harm than good by driving back the well-disposed at such a show of illiberality.

Close upon this squeamishness in regard to the pronouncement of Catholic doctrine follows an abhorrence of antagonizing the convictions of others, no matter how directly opposed to revealed truth, for with Liberal Catholics the most erroneous are as sacred as the truest convictions, being equally founded upon the principle of intellectual liberty. Thus they erect into a dogma what is called the principle of toleration. The differences of belief are, after all, they complacently argue, due to differences of temperament, education, etc.; we will not exactly approve them, but we should at least condone them.

The first conception of faith being naturalistic, in the development and application of that conception, either to the individual or to society, the same naturalistic element evolves itself. Hence it follows that the Liberal Catholic's appreciation of the Church has no foundation in its supernatural character. The Church does not address herself to his sympathies as a supernatural society whose first and supernatural end is the glory of God and the salvation of souls. It is on her social and human side that he regards her with affection. It is as the great civilizing and humanizing power which has lifted so many people from a state of barbarism, as the guardian of the ancient arts and letters, as the promoter of learning, that she wins his applause and approbation. She is first, not because she is first in herself by divine right, but first in virtue of the approval of his own great intellect. Under this false conception, apologies have been written in our times, and with strange inconsistency the Church is often lauded as the great promoter and preserver of civilization in the past, while her regressive tendencies are deplored in the presen; as if an institution, which alone, by divine constitution, has the perennial force of progress, could ever weaken or fail in her mission of human regeneration. Under the glamour of an advance towards the mirage of a false happiness in the desert of this life, our Liberal Catholics are proclaiming the shadow while rejecting the substance. True prog ress, which can only be achieved through an advance toward God, can never be effected save through that agency divinely appointed to lead us to God. This the Church of Jesus Christ alone can do, for she, under His institution, is as He Himself, the way, the truth, and the life.

Forgetting the divine and supernatural character of the Church (and she is nothing if not divine and supernatural), Liberal Catholics talk and write about her as a simple human development, accepting , in the blindness of their false conception, the naturalistic definition of faith. They thus eviscerate the Church, making her the mere husk of what she really is.

Piety itself does not escape the action of this pernicious naturalistic principle; it converts it into pietism--that is to say, into a parody of true piety, as is painfully seen in the pious practices of so many people who seek in their devotions only the sentimental emotions of which they themselves are able to be the source. They are devout over themselves, worshiping their own little sentiments and offering incense to idols graven after their own image. This is simply spiritual sensualism, and nothing else. Thus we see in our day in so many souls the degeneration of Christian asceticism (which is the purification of the heart by the repression of the appetites) and the falsification of Christian mysticism, which is neither emotion, nor interior consolation, nor any other epicurean foible of human sentiment, but union with God through a supernatural love for Him and through absolute submission to His holy will.

Therefore it is that the Catholicity of a great number of people in our times is a Liberal Catholicity, or rather, a false Catholicity. It is really not Catholicity, but mere naturalism, a pure rationalism; it is in a word paganism disguised in Catholic forms and using Catholic language.

Shadow And Penumbra

When we review the field of history in the vast stretch of time from the beginning of Christianity to our own day, the various heresies that have from time to time appeared seem clearly and distinctly marked off from the environment of the orthodox faith. We seem to be able to draw a geometrical line around about their respective areas, sharply dividing the camp of truth from that of error, separating the light from the darkness. But in this we are deceived; it is an illusion caused by distance. The distinction appears so clear, so definite only because we stand on the eminence of the present, from whose vantage ground we see, in large outline, the massed movements of peoples in the vast panorama of the past. A closer study, placing us in intellectual contact with these epochs, enables us to observe that never, in any period of history, were the dividing lines between truth and error defined with such geometrical exactness; not that, in reality, truth was not clearly and distinctly formulated in the definitions of the Church, but because, in its acceptation and its exterior profession by the generations of the past interested in these definitions, more or less confusion and looseness characterized their manner of taking them.

Error in society is like a stain upon some precious tissue. It is easily distinguished, but it is very difficult to define its limits. These limits are as indefinite as the twilight which merges the departing day into the coming night or as the dawn which blends the shadows of the spent darkness with the newborn light. So do the limits between error and truth in the actual affairs of men mingle in shadowy confusion. Error is a somber night; its limits fringe away from it like a huge penumbra, which is sometimes taken for the shadow itself, faintly brightened by some reflections of the dying light, or rather by the luminary yet enveloped and obscured by the first shades of evening.

So all error clearly formulated in Christian society is, as it were, surrounded by an atmosphere of the same error, but less dense, more rarified and tempered. Arianism had its Semi-Arianism, Pelagianism its Semi-Pelagianism, Lutherism its Jansenism, which was nothing else than a modified Lutherism. So in our own times, Liberalism has its Semi-Liberalism, which is nothing else than Catholic Liberalism. This is what the Syllabus terms modern Liberalism, that is, Liberalism without the boldness of its unvarnished first principles and stripped of the horrors of its last consequences; it is the Liberalism of those who are still unwilling not to appear to be Catholics or at least not to believe-- themselves Catholics. Liberalism is the baneful twilight of the truth, beginning to be obscured in their intelligence, or heresy, which has not yet taken complete possession of them.

On the other hand, we should not fail to note that there are those who are just emerging from the darkness of error into the twilight of truth. This class has not fully penetrated into the domain of truth. That they will ever enter the city of li ght depends upon their own sincerity and honesty. If they earnestly desire to know the truth in its fullness and seek it with sincere purpose, God's grace will not fail them. But they are in a dangerous position. On the borderland between the realms of light and darkness, the devil is most active and ingenious in detaining those who seem about to escape his snares, and he spares nothing to retain in his service a great number of people who would truly detest his infernal machinations if they only perceived them. His method, in the instance of persons infected with Liberalism, is to suffer them to place one foot within the domain of truth, provided they keep the other inside the camp of error. In this way they stand the victim of the devil's deceit and their own folly. In this way those whose consciences are not yet entirely hardened escape the salutary horrors of remorse; so the pusillanimous and the vacillating, who comprise the greater number of Liberals, avoid compromising themselves by pronouncing themselves such openly and squarely; so the shrewd and calculating according to the measure of expediency how much time they will spend in each camp, manage to show themselves the friends and allies of both; so a man is enabled to administer an official and recognized palliative to his failings, his weaknesses and his blunders. It is the obscurity that arises from the indefiniteness of clearly defined principles of truth and error in the Liberalist's mind that makes him the easy victim of Satan. His boasted strength is the very source of his weakness. It is because he has no real solid knowledge of the principles of truth and error that he is so easily deluded into the belief of his own intellectual superiority. He is in a mental haze--a fog which hides from him the abyss into which his vanity and pride, cunningly played upon by Satan, are invariably drawing him.

Two Kinds Of Liberalism

Philosophy and theology teach that there are two kinds of atheism, doctrinal or speculative and practical. The first consists in an open and direct denial of the existence of God; the second consists in acting and living without denying the existence of God, but yet as if He did not really exist. Those who profess the first are called theoretical or doctrinal atheists; those who live according to the second, practical atheists; the latter are the more numerous.

It is the same with Liberalism and Liberals. There are theoretical and practical Liberals. The first are the dogmatizers of the sect--the philosophers, the professors, the controversialists, the journalists. They teach Liberalism in books, in discourses, in articles, by argument or by authority, in conformity with a rationalistic criterion, in disguised or open opposition to the criterion of the divine and supernatural revelation of Jesus Christ.

Practical Liberalists are by far in the greater majority. Like a flock of sheep, with closed eyes, they follow their leaders. They know nothing in truth of principles and systems, and did they perceive the perversity of their instructors, would perhaps detest them. But, deceived by a false cry or shibboleth, they troop docilely after their false guides. They are none the less the hands that act, while the theorists are the heads that direct. Without them, Liberalism would never pass beyond the narrow bounds of speculation. It is the practical Liberalists that give it life and exterior movement. They constitute the prime matter of Liberalism--disposed to take on any form, ready for any folly or absurdity proposed by the leaders.

Amongst Catholic Liberals, many go to Mass, even make novenas, and yet when they come into contact with the world, they lead the lives of practical Liberals. They make it a rule "to live up to the times" as they call it. The Church they believe to be somewhat out-of-date, an old fogy, that she is held back by a certain set of reactionaries, ultramontanes; but they have hopes that she will in the course of time catch up with the modern spirit of progress, of which they are the van. The barnacles of medievalism still encumber the Bark of Peter, but time, they believe, will remedy this. The straw of medieval philosophy and theology they hope before long to thrash out by the introduction of the modern spirit into her schools. Then will a new theology be developed, more in conformity with the needs of the times, more in harmony with the modern spirit, which makes such large demands upon our "intellectual liberty". So they believe (or imagine they believe) that all is well. Is their responsibility before God therefore lessened? Assuredly not. They sin directly in the light of faith. They are less excusable than those Liberals who have never been within the pale of the Church. In short they sin with their eyes open.

Amongst Liberals we must not forget to include those who manage to evade any direct exposition or expression of the Liberal theory, but who nevertheless obliquely sustain it in their daily practice by writing and orating after the Liberal method, by recommending Liberal books and men, measuring and appreciating everything according to the Liberal criterion, and manifesting, on every occasion that offers, an intense hatred for anything that tends to discredit or weaken their beloved Liberalism. Such is the conduct of those prudent journalists whom it is difficult to apprehend in the flagrant advocacy of any proposition concretely Liberal, but who nevertheless, in what they say and in what they do not say, never cease to labor for the propagation of this cunning heresy. Of all Liberal reptiles, these are the most venomous.

Liberalism Of All Shades Condemned By The Church

Liberalism of every degree and all forms has been formally condemned--so much so that outside of the motives of its intrinsic malice, it stands under the formal ban of the Church, which is sufficient for all faithful Catholics. It would be impossible for an error so widespread and so radical to escape condemnation.

Upon its appearance in France at the time of the Revolution, the famous Declaration of the Rights of Man--which contains in germ all the follies of Liberalism--was condemned by Pius VI. Later, the baneful doctrine infected all the countries of Europe. In Spain it first took the name of Liberalism, under which it has since been known everywhere.

Upon the occasion of the appearance of the first errors of De Lamennais, Gregory XVI, in his encyclical Mirari Vos, explicitly condemned Liberalism as it was then understood, taught, and practiced by the constitutional governments of Europe. Later on, when the full tide of the deplorable deluge had submerged all Europe, carrying all before it, God raised up to His Church Pius IX, who has justly passed into history as the *Scourge of Liberalism*.

Liberal error, under all its forms, shapes, and shades, has been unmasked by this Pope. That his words might carry, as it were, more authority on this question, Providence has willed that these reiterated condemnations of Liberalism should fall from the lips of a Pontiff who, at the beginning of his pontificate, was hailed by Liberalists as their own. But he left no refuge to which their error might have resort. The numerous briefs and allocutions of Plus IX have clearly shown to Christian peoples what this baneful heresy is, and The Syllabus of Errors has put on the final seal of condemnation. Let us see the principal contents of some of the Pontifical documents. Amongst all that we might place before our readers, we will cite only a few.

On the 18th of June, 1871, responding to a deputation of French Catholics, Pius IX spoke thus:

"Atheism in legislation, indifference in matters of religion, and the pernicious maxims which go under the name of Liberal Catholicism are the true causes of the destruction of states; they have been the ruin of France. Believe me, the evil I denounce is more terrible than the Revolution, more terrible even than The Commune. I have always condemned Liberal Catholicism, and I will condemn it again forty times over if it be necessary."

In a brief, 6th of March, 1873, addressed to the Circle of St. Ambrose of Milan, the Sovereign Pontiff thus expresses himself:

"People are not wanting who pretend to form an alliance between light and darkness and to associate justice with iniquity in favor of those doctrines called Liberal Catholicism, which, based on the most pernicious principles, show themselves favorable to the intrusion of secular power upon the domain of spirituals; they lead their partisans to esteem, or at least to tolerate, iniquitous laws, as if it were not written that no one can serve two masters. Those who thus conduct themselves are more dangerous and more baneful than declared enemies, not only because, without being warned of it, perhaps even without being conscious of it, they second the projects of wicked men, but also because, keeping within certain limits, they show themselves with some appearance of probity and sound doctrine. They thus deceive the indiscreet friends of conciliation and seduce honest people, who would otherwise have strenuously combatted a declared error."

In the Brief of the 8th of May of the same year, speaking to the Confederation of the Catholic Circle of Belgium, the same Holy Father said:

"What we praise above all in your religious enterprise is the absolute aversion which, as we are informed, you show towards the principles of Liberal Catholicism and your intrepid determination to root them out as soon as possible. In truth you will extirpate the fatal root of discord and you will efficaciously contribute to unite and strengthen the minds of all in so combatting this insidious error, much more dangerous than an open enemy because it hides itself under the specious veil of zeal and of charity, and is so endeavoring to protect the people in general from its contaminating influence. Surely you, who adhere with such complete submission to all decisions of this Apostolic Seat and who know its frequent reprobations of Liberal principles, have no need of these warnings."

In the Brief to the La Croix, a Belgium journal, on the 24th of May, 1874, the Pope expresses himself thus:

"We cannot do less than to praise the design expressed in this letter, which we know your journal will satisfactorily fulfill, the design to publish, to spread, to comment on and inculcate in all minds all that the Holy See teaches against the perverse or at least false doctrines professed in so many quarters, and particularly against Liberal Catholicism, bitterly striving to conciliate light with darkness and truth with error."

On the 9th of June, 1873, Pius IX wrote to the president of the Council of the Catholic Association of Orleans, and without mentioning its name, depicts pietistic and moderated Liberalism in the following terms:

"Although you have not, strictly speaking, to combat impiety, are you not perhaps menaced on this side by as great dangers as those of the group of friends deceived by that ambiguous doctrine, which, while rejecting the last consequence of error, obstinately retains the germs, and which, not willing to embrace the truth in its fullness, and not daring to abandon it entirely, exhausts itself in interpreting the traditions and teachings of the Church by running them through the mold of its own private opinions."

In an address to the Bishop of Quimper, and speaking in reference to the general assembly of the Catholic Association of that diocese, the Pope said: "Assuredly these associations are not wanting in the obedience due to the Church, neither on account of the writings nor the actions of those who pursue them with invectives and abuse; but they might be pushed into the slippery path of error by the force of those opinions called Liberal; opinions accepted by many Catholics who are otherwise honest and pious, and who, even by the very influence which gives them their piety, are easily captivated and induced to profess the most pernicious maxims. Inculcate, therefore, Venerable Brother, in the minds of this Catholic assembly that, when we have so often rebuked the sectaries of these Liberal opinions, we have not had in view the declared enemies of the Church, whom it would have been idle to denounce, but rather that those of whom we are speaking are such as secretly guard the virus of Liberal principles which they have imbibed with their mother's milk. They boldly inoculate this virus into the people's minds, as if it were not impregnated with a manifest malice, and as if it were as harmless to religion as they think. They thus propagate the seed of those troubles which have held the world in revolution so long. Let them avoid these ambuscades. Let them endeavor to direct their blows against this perfidious enemy, and certainly they will merit much from their religion and their country."

With these utterances from the mouth of the Vicar of Jesus Christ our friends as well as our enemies must see that the Pope has said in diverse briefs, and particularly in the last citation, in a general way all that can be said on this question, which we are studying in its details.

The Solemn Condemnation Of Liberalism By The Syllabus

Liberalism has been condemned by the Pope in many and various documents. From these let us select a few epithets which stigmatize it with unsparing emphasis. They will bring out in striking relief the perfidious character of this cunning heresy.

In his Brief to Mgr. de Segur in regard to the latter's well-known work Hommage Aux Catholiques Liberaux, the Pope calls it a "perfidious enemy",-- in his allocution to the Bishop of Nevers, "the present real calamity"; in his letter to the Catholic Circle of St. Ambrose of Milan, "a compact between injustice and iniquity"; in the same document he speaks of it as "more fatal and dangerous than a declared enemy"; in his letter to the Bishop of Quimper, "a hidden poison"; in the brief to the Belgians, "a crafty and insidious error"; in another brief, to Mgr. Gaume, "a most pernicious pest." All these documents from which we quote may be found in full in Mgr. Segur's book, Hommage Aux Catholiques Liberaux.

But Liberalism is always strategically cunning. It rejected these very plain condemnations on the ground that they had all been made to private persons, that they were, therefore, of an entirely private character, by no means ex cathedra, and, of course, not binding. Heresy is always sophistically obstinate; it clings to the least pretext, seeks every excuse to escape condemnation. Barricading itself behind these technical defenses, Liberalism practically defied the authority of the Church. Its perfidy was short-lived. A solemn official public document of a general character and universally promulgated would sweep away the cobwebs with which Liberal Catholics had endeavored to bind the authority of the Sovereign Pontiff. The Church could not refuse a formal and decisive word to relieve the anxiety of her children. That word was spoken; it was The Syllabus of Errors, December 8, 1864.

All faithful Catholics hailed it with an enthusiasm only equaled in intensity by the paroxysm of fury with which the Liberals received it. Liberal Catholics thought it more prudent to strike at it covertly by overwhelming it with artificial interpretations. The Liberals denounced it with unsparing bitterness; the Liberal Catholics whittled it away by all manner of emasculating explanations. It was a document fatal to both; they had reason to fear it, the one execrating it, the other seeking with desperate subtlety to parry the blow, for the Syllabus is an official catalog of the principle errors of the day in the form of concrete propositions placed under the formal ban of the Church. In it will be found, succinctly formulated, the various errors which are met within the current literature of the times. The Syllabus crystallizes all these errors and stamps them with the seal of the explicit and formal condemnation of the Church. Here we have in detail all the Liberal dogmas. Although Liberalism may not be expressly named in any one of the propositions, most of its errors are there placed in pillory. From the condemnation of each of the Liberal errors results a condemnation of the whole system. Let us briefly enumerate them.

Condemnation of liberty of worship (propositions 15, 77 and 78); of the placet of governments (propositions 20 and 28); of the absolute supremacy of the State (proposition 38); of the secularization of public education (proposition 45, 40 and 48); of the absolute separation of Church and State (proposition 15); of the absolute right to legislate without regard to God (proposition 56); of the principle of non-intervention (proposition 62); of the right of insurrection (proposition 63); of civil marriage (proposition 73 and others); of the liberty (license) of the press (proposition 79); of universal suffrage as the source of authority (proposition 60); of even the name of Liberalism (proposition 88).

There have been books, pamphlets, and articles innumerable written on the proper interpretation of the propositions of the Syllabus. But the most authoritative interpretation ought to be that of its radical enemies, not of course in the absurdities of their misunderstandings or perversions, like Mr. Gladstone's unfortunate attempt to distort some of its propositions into a sanction of civil disloyalty, a position from which he has since withdrawn, we are glad to be able to say. But outside of such patent misconstructions, we may rely upon the interpretation given by Liberals of all shades, especially in those points wherein we see them wince under its uncompromising phraseology. When Liberals regard the Syllabus of Errors as their most detestable enemy, as the complete symbol of what they term Clericalism, Ultramontanism and Reaction, we may rest assured that it has been well interpreted in that quarter. Satan, bad as he is, is not a fool, and sees clearly enough where the blow falls with most effect. Thus, he has set the authority of his seal--which after God's is most reliable--on this great work, the seal of his inextinguishable hate. Here is an instance in which we can believe the Father of Lies. What he most abhors and defames possesses an unimpeachable guaranty of its truth.

Like Liberalism But Not Liberalism, Liberalism Bbut Not Like It

To effect a confusion of ideas is an old scheme of the devil. Not to understand clearly and precisely is generally the source of intellectual error. In time of schism and heresy, to cloud and distort the proper sense of words is a fruitful artifice of Satan, and it is as easy to lay snares for the intellectually proud as for the innocent. Every heresy in the Church bears testimony to Satan's success in deceiving the human intellect by obscuring and perverting the meaning of words. Arianism was a battle of words and owed its long-continued success to its verbal chicanery. Pelagianism and Jansenism showed the same characteristic, and today Liberalism is as cunning and obscure as any of its heretical predecessors.

For some, Liberalism consists in certain political forms; for others, in a certain tolerant and generous spirit opposed to despotism and tyranny; for others again it means simply civil equality; for many it becomes a vague and uncertain sentiment, which shapes itself into opposition to all arbitrary government. Although already defined, it will not be amiss to define Liberalism again.

In the first place, no political form of any kind whatsoever, whether democratic or popular, is of itself (ex se) Liberalism. Forms are mere forms and nothing more. Forms of government do not constitute their essence. Their forms are but their accidents. Their essence consists in the civil authority by virtue of which they govern, whether that authority be in form republican, democratic, aristocratic, monarchical; it may be an elective, hereditary, mixed or absolute monarchy. These various forms of themselves have nothing to do with Liberalism. Any one of them may be perfectly and integrally Catholic. If they accept beyond their own sovereignty the sovereignty of God, if they confess that they derive their authority from Him, if they submit themselves to the inviolable rule of the Christian law, if they hold for indisputable in their parliaments all that is defined by this law, if they acknowledge as the basis of public right the supreme morality of the Church and her absolute right in all things within her own competency, they are truly Catholic governments, whatever be their form, and the most exacting Ultramontanism cannot reproach them.

History offers the repeated example of republican powers which have been fervently Catholic. Such was the aristocratic republic of Venice; such the merchant republic of Genoa; such in our day are certain Swiss cantons. As examples of truly Catholic mixed monarchies, that of Catalognia and Aragon (the most democratic and at the same time the most Catholic of the Middle Ages), the ancient monarchy of Castile up to the advent of the House of Austria, the elective monarchy of Poland up to the time of the iniquitous dismemberment of that most religious realm. To believe that monarchies are of themselves (ex se) more religious than republics is an ignorant prejudice. The most scandalous examples of persecution against Catholicity in modern time have been given by monarchies; for instance, by Russia and by Prussia.

A government, whatever be its form, is Catholic if its constitution, its legislation, and its politics are based on Catholic principles; it is Liberal if it bases its constitution, its legislation, and its politics on rationalistic principles. It is not the act of legislation--by the king in a monarchy, by the people in a republic, or by both in a mixed form of government--which constitutes the essential nature of its legislation or of its constitution. What constitutes this is whether it does or does not carry with it the immutable seal of the Faith and whether it be or be not conformable with what the Christian law imposes upon states as well as upon individuals. just as amongst individuals, a king in his purple, a noble with his escutcheon or a workman in his overalls can be truly Catholic, so states can be Catholic, whatever be the place assigned them in the scale of governmental forms. In consequence, the fact of being Liberal or anti-Liberal has nothing whatever to do with the horror which everyone ought to entertain for despotism and tyranny, nor with the desire of civil equality between all citizens; much less with the spirit of toleration and of generosity, which, in their proper acceptation, are Christian virtues. And yet all this, in the language of certain people and of certain journals, is called Liberalism. Here we have an instance of a thing which has the appearance of Liberalism and which in reality is not Liberalism at all.

On the other hand, there exists a thing which is really Liberalism and yet has not the appearance of Liberalism. Let us suppose an absolute monarchy like that of Russia, or of Turkey, or better still, one of the conservative governments of our times, the most conservative imaginable; let us suppose that the constitution and the legislation of this monarchy or of this government is based upon the principle of the absolute and free will of the king or upon the equally unrestricted will of the conservative majority, in place of being based on the principles of Catholic right, on the indestructibility of the Faith, or upon a rigorous regard of the rights of the Church; then, this monarchy and this conservative government would be thoroughly Liberal and anti-Catholic. Whether the free-thinker be a monarch, with his responsible ministry, or a responsible minister, with his legislative corps, as far as consequences are concerned, it is absolutely the same thing. In both cases their political conduct is in the direction of free-thought, and therefore it is Liberal. Whether or not it be the policy of such a government to place restraints upon the freedom of the press; whether, no matter under what pretext, it grinds its subjects and rules with a rod of iron; a country so governed, though it will not be free, will without doubt be Liberal. Such were the ancient Asiatic monarchies; such are many of our modern monarchies; such was the government of Bismarck in Germany; such is the monarchy of Spain, whose constitution declares the king inviolable, but not God.

Here then we have something which, without seeming to resemble Liberalism, really is Liberalism, the more subtle and dangerous precisely because it has not the appearance of the evil it is.

We see, then, what care must be used in treating questions of this kind. It is of great importance above all that the terms of the discussion be carefully defined and that equivocations be studiously avoided which would favor error more than the truth.

The Name "Liberalism"

May a good Catholic take the term "Liberalism" in good part, and may he regard it creditable to be a Liberal? What harm, it may be urged, is there in the usage of these terms, as long as there is no actual acceptance of the Liberal creed. Why should not Catholics use the terms with a good sense injected into them? Let us see if there be validity in this claim.

It is certain that in the present age the word "Liberalism" signifies something not entirely in accord with true Catholicity. It cannot be said that we describe the situation in exaggerated terms. It must be admitted that in the current acceptation of the word, Liberalism and Catholic Liberalism have been explicitly condemned by Pius IX. Leaving aside for the moment those who pretend to profess a certain Liberalism without wishing it to be known as such, there is no doubt that the Liberalist current in Europe and America is anti-Catholic and rationalistic. Pass the world in review; what is meant by the Liberal party in Belgium, in France, in Germany, in Holland, in Austria, in Italy, in the South American Republics? Are they not anti-clerical, anti-Catholic? What is meant by their current language when they speak of the Liberal criterion: a Liberal atmosphere, Liberal thought, etc.? Look at the leaders of these parties, both in Europe and America; do not ninety-nine percent of them understand by Liberalism the application of a pure and mild rationalism, at least to social science? Do they not regard as their sole and most potent enemy what they contemptuously term Clericalism, Ultramontanism and do they not describe the Church as medieval, reactionary, the opponent of progress and the nurse of superstition? When then the term is so intimately associated with a Rationalism so radically opposed to the Church, how may Catholics use it with any hope of separating it from its current meaning?

In vain may some half dozen people imagine that they have given a different signification to a thing currently understood to bear the unmistakable stamp of anti-Catholicity. Beyond all dispute, common usage, the arbiter and judge of language, persists in regarding Liberalism as the implacable foe of Catholicity. In spite, then, of a thousand distinctions, exceptions and subtleties, you cannot fashion for yourself alone a Liberalism which has nothing contrary to the Faith in the opinion of most people, nor can you call yourself Liberal in any sense without being classed with all the other Liberals of that great family of Liberalism, such as the world understands it. The journal that seeks to be Catholic and at the same time has the name or reputation of Liberal becomes in the general opinion an ally of those who, under the Liberal banner, combat the Church in front and rear. Vainly will the editor of such a journal explain himself; his excuses and his explanations grow wearisome. To profess to be Catholic and yet subscribe himself to be Liberal is not the way to convince people of the sincerity of his profession. The editor of a journal purporting to be Catholic must be Catholic, not only in the profession he makes, but in spirit and in truth. To assume to be Liberal and then to endeavor to appear Catholic is to belie his faith; and although in his own heart he may imagine that he is as Catholic as the Pope (as several Liberals vaunt themselves), there is not the least doubt that his influence on current ideas and the march of events is thrown in favor of the enemy; and, in spite of himself, he becomes a satellite forced to move in the general orbit described by Liberalism.

And all this comes of a foolish desire to be estimated Liberal. Insane illusion! The usage of the word Liberal makes the Catholic who accepts it as his own one with all that finds shelter in its ominous shadow. Rationalism is the toadstool that flourishes in its dark shades, and with Rationalism does such a journalist identify himself, thus placing himself in the ranks of the enemies of Jesus Christ!

Moreover, there is little doubt that the readers of such journals are little prepared to distinguish the subtle limitations drawn by editors of this character between Liberalism and Liberalism. Most readers know the word in its common usage and class all things Liberal in a lump. When they see an ostensibly Catholic journal practically making common cause with the Liberal creed by sanctioning its name, they are easily led into the dangerous belief that Liberalism has some affinity with their faith, and this once engrafted in their minds, they become ready adepts of Rationalism.

Let us illustrate. There is in our day a sect which calls itself "The Old Catholics". Suppose that we, who are in the true sense of the word "old Catholics" "for our Catholicity dates from Calvary and the cenacle of Jerusalem, which are proofs of its antiquity, suppose we should establish a journal with the equivalent title: *Review of the Old Catholics*. Could it be said that this title is a lie? No, for we are old Catholics in the best sense of the words. But could it not be properly objected that this is a false-sounding title, inasmuch as it is in our day the cunning device of a schismatical sect? Certainly it would give occasion to well-informed Catholics to believe that we were schismatic and to the schismatics, who style themselves "Old Catholics" occasion to welcome us as new comrades in their rebellion against the Church. Why thus scandalize the faithful? But we use the word in a good sense. So be it! But would it not be better altogether to avoid the use of a term in so important a matter, which, under existing circumstances, is readily interpreted in a bad sense?

Now this is exactly the situation with those who consider inoffensive the term Liberal--reprobated by the Pope. Why should they take particular pains to employ a term requiring confusing explanations and which cannot but excite suspicion and cause scandal? Why rank themselves, for the sake of a term, with the enemy and carry his device--if, at bottom, they are Catholic? But it may be said that words are of little importance--why quibble in this way over the meaning of a term? We protest; words are of paramount importance, especially in our own day, when intellectual confusion so obscures fundamental truths in the modern mind. Words represent ideas. That is their value and their use. Modern error largely owes its success to its use of terms of an ambiguous character, or rather, by injecting a meaning into its words which hitherto carried a different signification. Agnosticism and Positivism have thus retained a Christian phraseology without the Christian meaning . They speak of God and sanctity and holiness and duty and freedom, but they have eviscerated the Christian meaning. Still these terms, with their former meanings, pass current in the public mind and so half-disguise the fatalism and paganism of the agnostic and positivist schools. Socialism has adopted the terms liberty, equality and fraternity as its watchwords, where in reality they mean revolution, destruction and "despotism. Yet it deceives the simple by thus disguising its real intent.

So has it always been. All heresies have begun in verbal disputes and ended in sanguinary conflicts of ideas. St. Paul exhorts Timothy to be on his guard, not only against false science ("Oppositiones falsi nominis scientiae"), but also against profane novelties of words ("profanas vocum novitates"). What would the Great Apostle of the nations say if today he saw Catholics decorating themselves with the title of Liberal, when that term stands in such violent and open antithesis to all that is Catholic? It is not merely a question Of words, but of what words represent. It is a question of truth and salvation. No, you cannot be a Liberal Catholic; incompatibles cannot be reconciled. You cannot assume this reprobated name, although you may be able by subtle sophisms to discover some secret way of reconciling it with your faith. Christian charity will not defend you, although you may repeatedly invoke it and would make it synonymous with the toleration of error. The first condition of charity is not to violate the truth, and charity cannot be the snare with which to surprise faith into the support of error. While we may admit the sincerity of those who are not Catholic, their error must always be held up to reprobation. We may pity them in their darkness, but we can never abet their error by i gnoring it or tolerating it. Beyond dispute, no Catholic can be consistently called "Liberal."

Most, however, to be feared is not he who openly boasts his Liberalism, but he who eschews the name and, vehemently denying it, is yet steeped to the lips in it and continually speaks and acts under its inspiration. And if such a man be a Catholic by profession, all the more dangerous is he to the faith of others, for he is the hidden enemy sowing tares amidst the wheat.

Liberalism And Free Thought

In our day the Catholic world, with as much justice as reason, attributes impiety as a quality of free-thought, whether in a person, a journal or an institution. "Free-thinker" is an odious epithet which few are willing to accept, but which many justly bear in spite of their protestations. They chafe under the appellation of the word, but find no inconvenience in being all that it implies. Persons, societies, books, governments which reject, in matters of faith and morals, the only and exclusive criterion--that of the Catholic Church--are Liberals. They acknowledge themselves to be Liberals. They feel honored to be so recognized and never dream of scandalizing anybody except us terrible "irreconcilables."

Now change the expression; instead of Liberals, call them free-thinkers. They resent the epithet as a calumny and grow indignant at the insult, as they term it. But why this excruciating tenderness, this delicate sensitiveness over the variations of a simple term? Have you not, dear friends, banished from your conscience, your books, your journals and your society all recognition of the supreme authority of the Church? Have you not raised up as the sole and fundamental criterion of your conduct and your thought your own untrammeled reason?

Very properly then do you say that you are Liberal, and no one will dispute the title with you. But you should remember that the very principle which makes you Liberal constitutes you free-thinkers. Every Liberal, no matter of what degree or shade, is ipso facto a freethinker, and every freethinker, as odious as the title may seem according to social conventionalities, is only a logical Liberal. He is simply a Liberal following his premises to their conclusions. This doctrine is as precise and as exact as a mathematical proposition. It is based on the laws of the strictest logic. It is a simple syllogism, whose premise is Liberalism and whose conclusion is free-thought.

Let us illustrate. You are a Catholic more or less open to false allurements, and as a punishment for your sins, you belong to a Liberal society, say, of a literary character. Consider a moment and ask yourself the following question: Would I continue to belong to this atheneum if tomorrow it should proclaim itself publicly and boldly a society of free-thought? What response would your conscience and your shame dictate? Would you not at once withdraw from its membership? As a Catholic you could take no part in its proceedings.

Again; you subscribe to a journal and read it without scruple, although it bears a Liberal title and speaks and reasons accordingly. Would you continue your subscription if all of a sudden it should place upon its title page the following heading: journal of Free-Thought. Well, this moderate or violent Liberal journal has been for years nothing more nor less than a free-thinker, and you have been imbibing its poison under the delusion of a word.

Ah! of how many prejudices would we rid ourselves if we only reflected a little on the meaning of words! Every society, whether scientific, literary or philanthropic, constituted on Liberal lines, is free-thinking. Every government Liberally organized is free-thinking. To reject with distrust the name and not the substance is blindness. Any institution, no matter what be its character, established in complete independence of the Magisterium of the Faith, is free-thinking . Catholics cannot, consistently with their faith, belong to them. Membership there means rebellion against the Church.

In all such institutions Liberalism rei gns and, in consequence, free-thought. No Catholic can remain a Catholic and affiliate with them. We are Catholics all-in-all--or not at all. We cannot dwell in an atmosphere where God is not. There is no true spiritual life where Jesus Christ is not, and He has given His promise to be with His Church forever. He who abides not in Him lives in the outer darkness.

How much do perverse Catholics serve the devil by obstinately clinging to such associations and participating in their works! In the folly of their ignorance, which they assert against the wisdom of the Church, they harden their consciences to the practical guidance of the Holy See and blindly enlist in the service of an enemy whose cunning deludes them into the slavery of Hell--under the disguise of freedom! They forget that the Truth alone makes them free. To know and serve God is the only freedom, and Liberalism completely severs the bond which links man to God. With a just and rational horror does a good Catholic regard Liberalism. Ultramontanism will never cause you to loose your soul; Liberalism is a broad road to the infernal abyss.

Can a Liberal Be In Good Faith?

Is there such a thing in rerum natura ["in the nature of things"] as a Liberal in good faith? In our day it seems almost impossible to reconcile Liberalism with good faith, which is the only thing that can give it the shadow of excuse. It cannot, however, be denied that, absolutely speaking, there may exist under peculiar circumstances an exceptional case, but this will indeed be unique.

In the history of heresy we frequently find some individuals, even many, who, in spite of themselves, are dragged into the torrent of error for no other reason than their supreme ignorance. But it must be admitted that, if ever an error has been deprived of any excuse on this score, that error is Liberalism as it exists today. Most heresies which have rent the bosom of the Church have attempted to disguise their errors under an exterior of affected piety. Jansenism, perhaps the most subtle of all heresies, won over a great number of adherents by its cunning simulation of sanctity. Its morals were rigid to the extreme; its dogmas formidable; the exterior conduct of its promoters ascetic and apparently enlightened. It wore the visage of a Saint, while at heart it reeked with the corruption of pride. The majority of ancient heresies turned upon very subtle points of doctrine, which only the skilled theologian could discern, and upon which the ignorant multitude could give no judgment, save such as they received in confidence from their leaders. By a very natural consequence, when the hierarchy of a diocese fell into error, most of his subordinates--clerics and laity full of confidence in their pastor--fell with him. This was all the easier, owing to the difficulty of communication with Rome in ancient times, when the infallible voice of the Universal Pastor could not readily reach the flock in parts remote from the Chair of Peter. The diffusion of many ancient heresies, which were mostly purely theological, was nearly always due to this cause. Hence we find St. Jerome crying out in the fourth century: Ingemuit universus orbis se esse Arianum: "The whole world groaned to find itself Arian." This also explains how in the midst of great schisms and great heresies, such as the Greek Schism and Anglican heresy, there may be numbers of souls in whom the roots of the True Faith are not dead, although in its exterior profession this faith may appear deformed and vicious. Such was the case in England for many years after the rebellion of Henry VIII, and such, in some instances, is the case in our own times, for the ready acceptance of the True Faith by many English converts of recent years bears ample witness to the vitality of the Faith in souls so grossly betrayed into heresy by apostate guides three centuries ago. Such souls, united to the Mystical Body of the Church by Baptism, by interior Sanctifying Grace, are able to gain eternal salvation with ourselves.

Can the same be said of Liberalism?

Liberalism first presented itself under a political mask, but since its debut, this mask has become so transparent that blind indeed is he who cannot divine the perversity of such a miserable travesty. The veil of hypocrisy and pietism which some of its panegyrists first threw around it has been stripped off. The halo in which it was first depicted has shown itself to be, not the soft light of Heaven, but the lurid glare of Hell. It has gathered under its banner all the dregs of society, wherever corruption was its precursor and promoter.

The new doctrines which it preached--and which it wished to substitute for ancient truth--had nothing abstract nor metaphysical; it rejected everything but brutal facts, which betrayed it as the offspring of Satan and the enemy of mankind. The terrors of the French Revolution were the evidence of its origin, as sprung from the corruptions of a society that had abandoned God and battened on the bestial results of Voltarian skepticism. No wonder it avoided the abstract and the metaphysical, to revel in the atrocious deeds of a bloody revolution, which proclaimed the absolute sovereignty of man against his Creator and the Church.

If such were the horrors of the birth of Liberalism, what must be said of its odious development in our own day, when its infernal principles bask in the full light of the world's approbation? Never has an error been more severely castigated by the condemnation of the Church; never more accurately have those condemnations been borne out by the testimony of experience and history. When Protestantism is fast losing its power, sinking into the abyss out of sheer impotence, Liberalism, even more formidable and more dangerous, fills the ranks of this decaying heresy with enemies still more resourceful, implacable and obstinate. Protestantism is now a dead dog; Liberalism a living lion going about seeking whom he may devour. Its dreadful doctrine is permeating society to the core; it has become the modern political creed and threatens us with a second revolution, to turn the world over once again to paganism. Are there any good Catholics who do not believe this? Let them but read the signs of the times, not with the eyes of the world, but by the light of the Faith, which Jesus Christ gave to them. "I am the way, the truth and the life," said our Divine Lord. "He that followeth me, walketh not in darkness, but shall have the li ght of life." (John 8:12). He who follows the Church follows Him, for He Himself said to the Apostles and their successors, "He who hears you, hears Me."

What then is the attitude of the Church towards Liberalism? Is not its entire hierarchy considered hostile to Liberalism? Does not Liberalism itself bear witness to this? What does the word "Clericalism" with which the Liberals have honored those most energetically opposed to their doctrine, prove, if not that they regard the Church as their most implacable adversary? How do they look upon the Pope, upon bishops, priests, religious of all kinds, on pious people and practical Catholics? "Clericals" "clericals" always, that is, "anti-Liberals!"

How then can we expect to find good faith on the part of a Liberal Catholic when orthodoxy is so distinctly and completely opposed to Liberalism? Those who are capable of comprehending the principles of the question can readily satisfy themselves on its merits by its intrinsic reasons; those who cannot so comprehend have an extrinsic authority more than sufficient to form an accurate judgment for them, such as it should be in every good Christian in matters touching the Faith. Light is not wanting; those who will, can see well enough. But alas! Insubordination, illegitimate interests and the desire to take and make things easy are abundantly at hand to prejudice and to blind. The seduction of Liberalism is not of the kind that blinds by a false light, but rather by the seduction which, in sullying the heart, obscures the understanding . We may therefore justly believe, except perhaps with very rare exception, that it requires a very vigorous effort of charity to admit in our day, in accordance with true moral principles, the excuse of "good faith" in a Catholic who entertains Liberal principles.

The Symptoms Of Liberalism

What are the signs or symptoms by which we may distinguish what is and what is not Liberalism in a person, a journal, a book or an institution? We are surrounded by Liberalism in all its shapes and varieties, and it behooves us to be on our guard against its subtle dangers. To lay down special rules by which we may detect it in its shadings and minutiae is neither practical nor necessary. But some general directions may be given. Their application must be left to each one's proper discretion.

To facilitate the matter, we will divide Liberals, whether persons or writings, into three classes: 1) Extreme Liberals; 2) Moderate Liberals; 3) Quasi Liberals, or those only tainted with Liberalism.

We will essay a description of each of these types. The study of their physiognomy will not be without interest and profit, for in the types we shall find a rule for our guidance in distinguishing Liberalism in its practical details.

The Extreme Liberal is easily recognized; he does not attempt to deny or conceal his perversity. He is the declared enemy of the Pope, of priests, of everything ecclesiastical; a thing has only to be sacred to rouse his implacable wrath; priestcraft is his favorite shibboleth. He subscribes to all the most violent and incendiary journals, the more impious and blasphemous, the better to his liking. He is ready to go to the furthermost conclusions of his baneful system. His premise of destruction once laid down, his conclusion of nihilism is a mere matter of logic. He would put it into practical execution with pleasure and exultation if circumstances permitted. He is a revolutionist, socialist, anarchist. He glories in living a life devoid of all religion. He belongs to secret societies, dies in their embrace and is buried by their ritual. He has always defied religion and dies in his defiance.

The moderate Liberal is just as bad as his extreme confrere, but he takes good care not to appear so. Social conventionalities and good manners are everything to him; these points secured, the rest is of little importance. Provided his iniquity is kid-gloved, it finds ready extenuation in his own mind. The niceties of polite society preserved, his Liberalism knows no bounds. He would not burn a convent--that would appear too brutal, but the convent once burned, he has no scruple in seizing upon the outraged property. The cheap impiety of a penny paper grates on his well-bred nerves; the vulgar blasphemy of Ingersoll he deprecates; but let the same impiety and the same blasphemy appear in the columns of a so-called reputable journal, or be couched in the silken phraseology of a Huxley in the name of science, and he applauds the polished sin. It is with him a question of manner, not matter. At the mere mention of the name of a nihilistic or socialistic club, he is thrown into a cold sweat, for there, he declares, the masses are seduced into principles which lead to the destruction of the foundations of society; yet, according to him, there is no danger, no inconvenience in a free lyceum where the same principles are elegantly debated and sympathetically applauded; for who could dare to condemn the scientific discussion of social problems? The moderate Liberal does not detest the Pope; he may even express admiration for his sagacity; he only blames certain pretensions of the Roman Curia and certain exaggerations of Ultramontanism, which do not fall in with the trend of modern thought. He may even like priests, above all, those who are enlightened, that is, such as have caught the twang of modern progress; as for fanatics and reactionaries, he simply avoids or pities them. He may even go to Church and, stranger still, sometimes approach the Sacraments; but his maxim is, in the Church to live as a Christian, outside of the Church to live as the world lives, according to the times in which one is born and not obstinately to swim against the stream. He dies with the priest on one side, his infidel literature on the other and imagines that his Creator will applaud his breadth of mind.

The Catholic simply tainted with Liberalism is generally a good man and sincerely pious; he exhales nevertheless an odor of Liberalism in everything he says, writes, or takes up. Like Madame de Sevi gne, he can say, "I am not the rose, but standing by it, I have caught some of its perfume" This courageous man reasons, speaks, and acts as a Liberal without knowing it. His strong point is charity; he is charity itself. What horror fills his soul at the exaggerations of the Ultramontane press! To treat as a liar the man who propagates false ideas is, in the eyes of this singular theologian, to sin against the Holy Spirit. To him the falsifier is simply misguided; it is not the poor fellow's fault; he has, simple soul, been misled. We ought neither to resist nor combat him; we must strive to attract him by soft words and pretty compliments. How the devil must chuckle over the mushy charity held out as a bait to abet his own cause! To smother evil under an abundance of good is the tainted Catholic's favorite maxim, read one day by chance in Balmes, and the only thing he has ever retained of the great Spanish philosopher. From the Gospel he is careful to cite only those texts flavored with milk and honey. The terrible invectives of Our Lord against Pharisaism astonish and confound him; they seem to be an excess of language on the part of our Divine Savior! He reserves these denunciatory texts to use against those provoking Ultramontanes who every day compromise, by their exaggerated and harsh language, the cause of a religion that he thinks should be all peace and love. Against them his Liberalism, ordinarily so sweet and gentle, grows bitter and violent. Against them his zeal flames up, his polemics grow sharp, and his charity becomes aggressive. In a celebrated discourse delivered apropos certain accusations against Louis Veuillot, Pere Felix once cried out, "Gentlemen, let us love and respect even our friends." But no, our Catholic tainted with Liberalism will do nothing of the kind. He saves the treasures of his tolerance and his charity for the sworn enemies of the Faith! What is more natural? Does not the poor man want to attract them? On the other hand, for the most heroic defenders of the Faith, he has only sarcasm and invective.

In short, the tainted Catholic cannot comprehend that direct opposition, per diametrum, of which St. Ignatius speaks in his Spiritual Exercises. He does not know how to give a direct blow. He knows no other tactics than to attack on the flank, tactics which, in religion, may perhaps be convenient, but are never decisive. He wants to conquer, but on the condition of not wounding the enemy, of never disturbing his ease or his rest. The mere mention of war painfully agitates his nerves and rouses all his pacific dispositions. With the enemy in full assault, with the implacable hatred and cunning of falsehood almost sweeping over him he would withstand the hostile charge and stem the overwhelming tide with the paper barriers of an illusive peace.

In a word, we may recognize the extreme and the moderate Liberal by his bitter fruits; the tainted Catholic may be recognized by his distorted affection for Liberalism and its works.

The extreme Liberal roars his Liberalism; the moderate Liberal mouths it; the tainted Catholic whispers and sighs it. All are bad enough and serve the devil well. Nevertheless, the extreme Liberal overreaches himself by his violence; the fecundity of the tainted Catholic is partially sterilized by his hybrid nature; but the moderate is the real Satanic type; his is the masked evil, which in our times is the chief cause of the ravages of Liberalism.

Christian Prudence And Liberalism

Owing to their circumstances, Catholics in this country live in the very midst of Liberalism; we are surrounded by and come into daily contact with extreme and moderate Liberals, as well as with Catholics tainted with its all-pervading poison. So did Catholics in the fourth century live among Arians, those of the fifth among Pelagians, and those of the seventeenth amongst Jansenists. It is impossible not to sustain some relations with the Liberals who surround us; we meet them everywhere--in our social dealings, in our business affairs, in our amusements and pleasures, even in Church and in the family. How then shall we comport ourselves in our unavoidable intercourse with those who are thus spiritually diseased? How may we avoid contagion, or at least diminish the risk to a minimum?

To lay down a precise rule for every case is a difficulty beyond human capacity, but some general rules of guidance may be given; their application must be left to the prudence of those who are individually concerned, according to their circumstances and special obligations. It will be well first to distinguish, in a general way, three possible relations between a Catholic and Liberalism, or rather between a Catholic and Liberals: 1) Necessary relations; 2) Useful relations; 3) Relations of pure affection or pleasure.

Necessary relations are imposed upon everyone by his station in life and his particular position; they cannot be avoided. Such are the family relations, the relations of inferior and superior, etc.

It is evident that a son who has the misfortune to have a Liberal father cannot on this account abandon him, nor the wife the husband, the brother the sister, nor the parent the child, except in the case where their Liberalism exacts from any of their respective inferiors acts essentially opposed to religion, so as to conduce to a formal apostasy.

But it will not suffice, on the part of a Catholic, for the taking of such a step that mere restraint is put upon his liberty in the performance of the precepts of the Church. For we must remember that the Church places no obligation in such matters on a person who could only perform them under grave inconvenience (sub gravi incommodo).

The Catholic unfortunate enough to be so placed must bear with Christian patience his painful situation and surround himself, as far as lies in his power, with every precaution to avoid the contagion of bad example in word or deed. Prayer should be his chief recourse, prayer for himself and the victims of error. He should avoid, as far as possible, all conversations on this topic, but when he finds that a controversy is thrust upon him, let him accept it in the full confidence of the truth, and armed with effective weapons of defense and offense. A prudent spiritual director should be consulted in the selection of his arsenal. As an antidote to much association with Liberals, let him frequent the company of other persons of science and authority who are in the constant possession of sound doctrine. Obedience to a superior in all that is not directly or indirectly against faith and morals is his bounden duty, but it is equally his duty to refuse obedience to anything directly or indirectly in opposition to the integrity of his faith. Courage he can draw only from supernatural sources; God, who sees the struggle, will not refuse all the assistance needed.

There are other relations which we have with Liberals, which are not absolutely, but which are morally indispensable, and without which social life, which consists in a mutual exchange of services, is impossible. Such are the relations of commerce, trade, labor, the professions, etc. But that strict subjection, which holds under the necessary relations of which we have just been speaking, does not exist here, and in consequence, one can exercise more independence. The fundamental rule in these cases is not to enter into unnecessary intercourse; what the gearing of the social machine demands, and no more, is sufficient. If you are a merchant, buy and sell with Liberals in accordance with the needs of your business; more than this, avoid; if you are a domestic, limit your intercourse to the necessities of your service; if you are a laborer, to giving and receiving what is due on either part. Guided by these rules, one could live without injury to his faith amidst a population of Jews. At the same time, it should never be forgotten that any manifestation of weakness or compromise is never needed. Even Liberals cannot refuse respect to the man who stands firmly and unflinchingly in his conviction, and when the Faith is in question, despicable in all men's eyes does he become who would sell his birthright for a mess of pottage.

Relations of pure friendship, pleasure or affectation, which we enter into as mere matters of taste or inclination, should be eschewed and, if once contracted, ought to be voluntarily broken off. Such relations are a certain danger to our faith. Our Lord says that he who loves danger shall perish in it. Is it difficult to sever such connections? What if it is; we must burst the bonds that place us in peril. Reflect for a moment. If your Liberal companion with whom you are constantly associating were subject to some contagious disease, would you then court him? If your relations with him compromised your reputation, would you continue them? If he were to asperse [attack] your family, would you cling to him still? Well, the honor of God and your own spiritual safety are at stake in this matter; what human prudence would counsel you to do for your worldly interest and human honor, surely that much at least your spiritual interests require from you. There is but one condition upon which intimacy with a Liberal is justifiable at all, and that is for the purpose of converting him. For this, two dispositions are necessary: your Liberal friend's willingness and your capacity to lead him to the light. Even here danger is not lacking. One must be very sure of his ground before he attempts the task.

Above all, have a horror of heresy, and Liberalism today is the most mali gnant of all heresies. Its face is absolutely set against religious faith. The first thing to do in an infected country is to isolate oneself, and if this is not possible, take all sanitary precautions against the deadly germ. Spiritual health is always endangered whenever we come into contact with Liberalism, and infection is almost certain if we neglect those precautions which prudence suggests.

Liberalism And Literature

Liberalism is a system, as Catholicism is, although in a contrary sense. It has its arts, its science, its literature, its economics, its ethics; that is, it has an organism all its own, animated by its own spirit and distinguishable by its own physiognomy. The most powerful heresies, for instance, Arianism in ancient times and Jansenism in our own days, presented like peculiarities.

Not only are there Liberal journals, but there exists a literature in all the shades and degrees of Liberalism; it is abundant and prolific. The present generation draws its main intellectual nourishment from it. Our modern literature is saturated with its sentiments, and for this reason should we take every precaution to guard against its infections, of which so many are the miserable victims. How is it to be avoided?

The rules of guidance in this case are analogous to or almost identical with the rules which should govern a Catholic in his personal relations with Liberals, for books are after all but the representatives of their authors, conveying by the printed, instead of the spoken word, what men think, feel and say. Apply to books those rules of conduct which should regulate our intercourse with persons, and we have a safeguard in reading the literature of the day. But in this instance, the control of the relation is practically in our own power, for it depends entirely on ourselves whether we seek or tolerate the reading of Liberal books. They are not apt to seek us out, and if they are thrust upon us, our consent to their perusal is practically all our own doing. We have none but ourselves to blame if they prove to be our own undoing.

There is one point, however, worthy of our close consideration. It should be a fundamental rule in a Catholic's intellectual life. It is this: Spare your praises of Liberal books, whatever be their scientific or literary merit, or at least praise with great reserve, never forgetting the reprobation rightly due to a book of Liberal spirit or tendency. This is an important point. It merits the strictest attention. Many Catholics, by far too naive (even some engaged in Catholic journalism), are perpetually seeking to pose as impartial and are perpetually daubing themselves with a veneer of flattery. They lustily beat the bass drum and blow all the trumpets of their vocabulary in praise of no matter what work, literary or scientific, that comes from the Liberal camp. They are fearful of being considered narrow-minded and partial if they do not give the devil his due. In the fulsomeness of their flattery, they hope to show that it costs a Catholic nothing to recognize merit wherever it may be found; they imagine this to be a powerful means of attracting the enemy. Alas, the folly of the weaklings; they play a losing game; it is they who are insensibly attracted, not the enemy! They simply fly at the bait held out by the cunning fisher who satanically guides the destinies of Liberalism.

Let us illustrate. When Arnold's Light of Asia appeared, not a few Catholics joined in the chorus of fulsome praise which greeted it. How charming, how beautiful, how tender, how pathetic, how humane; what lofty morality, what exquisite sentiment! Now what was the real purport of the book and what was its essence? To lift up Guatama, the founder of Buddhism, at the expense of Jesus Christ, the Founder of Christianity! The intention was to show that Guatama was equally a divine teacher with as high an aspiration, as great a mission, as lofty a morality as our Divine Lord Himself. This was the object of the book; what was its essence? A falsification of history by weaving a series of poetical legends around a character, about whose actual life practically nothing is known. But not only this, the character was built up upon the model of Our Lord, which the author had in his own mind as the precious heirloom of Christianity; and his Guatama, whom he intended to stand out as at least the divine equal of the Founder of Christianity, became in his hands in reality a mere echo of Christ, the image of Christ, made to rival the Word made flesh! Buddhism, in the borrowed garments of Christianity, was thus made to appeal to the ideals of Christian peoples, and gaining a footing in their admiration and affections, to usurp the throne in the Christian sanctuary. Here was a work of literary merit, although it has been greatly exaggerated in this respect, praised extravagantly by some Catholics who, in their excessive desire to appear impartial, failed or refused to see in Edwin Arnold's Light of Asia a most vicious, anti-Christian book!

What difference does it make whether a book be excellent in a literary sense or not, if its effect be the loss of souls and not their salvation? What if the weapon in the hands of the assassin be bright or not, if it be fatal? Though spiritual assassination be brilliant, it is nonetheless deadly. Heresy under a charming disguise is a thousand times more dangerous than heresy exposed in the harsh and arid garb of the scholastic syllogism-- through which the death's skull grins in unadorned hideousness. Arianism had its poets to propagate its errors in popular verse. Lutheranism had its humanists, amongst whom the elegant Erasmus shone as a brilliant writer. Arnauld, Nicole, Pascal threw the glamour of their belles letters over the serpentine doublings of Jansenism. Voltaire's wretched infidelity won its frightful popularity from the grace of his style and the flash of his wit. Shall we, against whom they aimed the keenest and deadliest shafts, contribute to their name and their renown! Shall we assist them in fascinating and corrupting youth! Shall we crown these condemners of our faith with the laurels of our praises and laud them for the very qualities which alone make them dangerous! And for what purpose? That we may appear impartial? No. Impartiality is not permissible when it is distorted to the offense of truth, whose ri ghts are imprescriptible. A woman of bad life is infamous, be she ever so beautiful, and the more beautiful, the more dangerous. Shall we praise Liberal books out of gratitude? No! Follow the liberals themselves in this, who are far more prudent than we; they do not recommend and praise our books, whatever they be. They, with the instinct of evil, fully appreciate where the danger lies. They either seek to discredit us or to pass us by in silence.

Si quis non amat Dominum Nostrum Jesum Christum, Sit anathema ["If anyone does not love the Lord Jesus Christ, let him be anathema"], says St. Paul. Liberal literature is the written hatred of Our Lord and His Church. If its blasphemy were open and direct, no Catholic would tolerate it for an instant; is it any more tolerable because, like a courtesan, it seeks to disguise its sordid features by the artifice of paint and powder?

Charity And Liberalism

Narrow! Intolerant! Uncompromising! These are the epithets of odium hurled by Liberal votaries of all degrees at us Ultramontanes. Are not Liberals our neighbors like other men? Do we not owe to them the same charity we apply to others? Are not your vigorous denunciations, it is urged against us, harsh and uncharitable and in the very teeth of the teaching of Christianity, which is essentially a religion of love? Such is the accusation continually flung in our face. Let us see what its value is. Let us see all that the word "Charity" signifies.

The Catechism, that popular and most authoritative epitome of Catholic theology, gives us the most complete and succinct definition of charity; it is full of wisdom and philosophy. Charity is a supernatural virtue which induces us to love God above all things and our neighbors as ourselves for the love of God. Thus, after God we ought to love our neighbor as ourselves, and this not just in any way, but for the love of God and in obedience to His law. And now, what is it to love? Amare est velle bonum, replies the philosopher. "To love is to wish good to him whom we love." To whom does charity command us to wish good? To our neighbor, that is to say, not to this or that man only, but to everyone. What is that good which true love wishes? First of all supernatural good, then goods of the natural order which are not incompatible with it. All this is included in the phrase "for the love of God."

It follows, therefore, that we can love our neighbor when displeasing him, when opposing him, when causing him some material injury, and even, on certain occasions, when depriving him of life; in short, all is reduced to this: Whether in the instance where we displease, oppose, or humiliate him, it is or is not for his own good, or for the good of someone whose rights are superior to his, or simply for the greater service of God.

If it is shown that in displeasing or offending our neighbor we act for his good, it is evident that we love him, even when opposing or crossing him. The physician cauterizing his patient or cutting off his gangrened limb may nonetheless love him. When we correct the wicked by restraining or by punishing them, we do nonetheless love them. This is charity--and perfect charity.

It is often necessary to displease or offend one person, not for his own good, but to deliver another from the evil he is inflicting. It is then an obligation of charity to repel the unjust violence of the aggressor; one may inflict as much injury on the aggressor as is necessary for defense. Such would be the case should one see a highwayman attacking a traveler. In this instance, to kill, wound, or at least take such measures as to render the aggressor impotent, would be an act of true charity.

The good of all good is the divine Good, just as God is for all men the Neighbor of all neighbors. In consequence, the love due to a man, inasmuch as he is our neighbor, ought always to be subordinated to that which is due to our common Lord. For His love and in His service we must not hesitate to offend men. The deg ree of our offense towards men can only be measured by the degree of our obligation to Him. Charity is primarily the love of God, secondarily the love of our neighbor for God's sake. To sacrifice the first is to abandon the latter. Therefore, to offend our neighbor for the love of God is a true act of charity. Not to offend our neighbor for the love of God is a sin.

Modern Liberalism reverses this order; it imposes a false notion of charity: our neighbor first, and, if at all, God afterwards. By its reiterated and trite accusations toward us of intolerance, it has succeeded in disconcerting even some staunch Catholics. But our rule is too plain and too concrete to admit of misconception. It is this: Sovereign Catholic inflexibility is sovereign Catholic charity. This charity is practiced in relation to our neighbor when, in his own interest, he is crossed, humiliated, and chastised. It is practiced in relation to a third party when he is defended from the unjust aggression of another, as when he is protected from the contagion of error by unmasking its authors and abettors and showing them in their true light as iniquitous and pervert, by holding them up to the contempt, horror, and execration of all. It is practiced in relation to God when, for His glory and in His service, it becomes necessary to silence all human considerations, to trample under foot all human respect, to sacrifice all human interests--and even life itself--to attain this highest of all ends. All this is Catholic inflexibility and inflexible Catholicity in the practice of that pure love which constitutes soverei gn charity. The Saints are the types of this unswerving and sovereign fidelity to God, the heroes of charity and religion. Because in our times

61

there are so few true inflexibles in the love of God, so also are there few uncompromisers in the order of charity. Liberal charity is condescending, affectionate, even tender in appearance, but at bottom it is an essential contempt for the true good of men, of the supreme interests of truth and of God. It is human self love, usurping the throne of the Most High and demanding that worship which belongs to God alone.

Polemical Charity And Liberalism

Liberalism never gives battle on solid ground; it knows too well that in a discussion of principles it must meet with irretrievable defeat. It prefers tactics of recrimination and, under the sting of a just flagellation, whiningly accuses Catholics of lack of charity in their polemics. This is also the ground which certain Catholics, tainted with Liberalism, are in the habit of taking.

Let us see what is to be said on this score. We Catholics, on this point as on all others, have reason on our side; whereas, Liberals have only its shadow. In the first place, a Catholic can handle his Liberal adversary openly, if such he be in truth; no one can doubt this. If an author or a journalist make open profession of Liberalism and does not conceal his Liberal predilections, what injury can be done him in calling him a Liberal? Si palam res est, repetitio injuria non est: "To say what everybody knows is no injury." With much stronger reason, to say of our neighbor what he every instant says of himself cannot justly offend. And yet, how many Liberals, especially those of the easy-going and moderate type, regard the expressions "Liberal" and "friend of Liberals" which Catholic adversaries apply to them, as offensive and uncharitable!

Granting that Liberalism is a bad thing, to call the public defenders and professors of Liberalism bad is no want of charity.

The law of justice, potent in all ages, can be applied in this case. The Catholics of today are no innovators in this respect. We are simply holding to the constant practice of antiquity. The propagators and abettors of heresy, as well as its authors, have at all times been called heretics. As the Church has always considered heresy a very grave evil, so has she always called its adherents bad and pervert. Run over the list of ecclesiastical writers-you will then see how the Apostles treated the first heretics, how the Fathers and modern controversialists and the Church herself in her official language has pursued them. There is then no sin against charity in calling evil evil; its authors abettors and its disciples bad; all its acts, words, and writings iniquitous, wicked, malicious. In short, the wolf has always been called the wolf; and in so calling it, no one ever has believed that wrong was done to the flock and the shepherd.

If the propagation of good and the necessity of combating evil require the employment of terms somewhat harsh against error and its supporters, this usage is certainly not against charity. This is a corollary or consequence of the principle we have just demonstrated. We must render evil odious and detestable. We cannot attain this result without pointing out the dangers of evil, without showing how and why it is odious, detestable and contemptible. Christian oratory of all ages has ever employed against impiety the most vigorous and emphatic rhetoric in the arsenal of human speech. In the writings of the great athletes of Christianity, the usage of irony, imprecation, execration and of the most crushing epithets is continual. Hence the only law is the opportunity and the truth.

But there is another justification for such usage. Popular propagation and apologetics cannot preserve elegant and constrained academic forms. In order to convince the people, we must speak to their heart and their imagination, which can only be touched by ardent, brilliant, and impassioned language. To be impassioned is not to be reprehensible-when our heat is the holy ardor of truth.

The supposed violence of modern Ultramontane journalism not only falls short of Liberal journalism, but is amply justified by every page of the works of our great Catholic polemists of other epochs. This is easily verified. St. John the Baptist calls the Pharisees a "race of vipers"; Jesus Christ, Our Divine Savior, hurls at them the epithets "hypocrites, whitened sepulchres, a per-verse and adulterous generation," without thinking for this reason that He sullies the sanctity of His benevolent speech. St. Paul criticizes the schismatic Cretians as "always liars, evil beasts, slothful bellies." The same Apostle calls Elymas the magician a "Seducer, full of guile and deceit, a child of the devil, an enemy of all justice."

If we open the Fathers, we find the same vigorous castigation of heresy and heretics. St. Jerome, arguing against Vigilantius, casts in his face his former occupation of saloon-keeper: "From your infancy," he says to him, "you have learned other things than theology and betaken yourself to other pursuits. To verify at the same time the value of your money accounts and the value of Scriptural texts, to sample wines and grasp the meaning of the prophets and apostles are certainly not occupations which the same man can accomplish with credit." On another occasion, attacking the same Vigilantius, who denied the excellence of virginity and of fasting , St. Jerome, with his usual sprightliness, asks him if he spoke thus "in order not to diminish the receipts of his saloon?" Heavens! what an outcry would be raised if one of our Ultramontane controversialists were to write against a Liberal critic or heretic of our own day in this fashion!

What shall we say of St. John Chrysostom? Is his famous invective against Eutropius not comparable, in its personal and aggressive character, to the cruel invectives of Cicero against Catiline and against Verres! The gentle St. Bernard did not honey his words when he attacked the enemies of the Faith. Addressing Arnold of Brescia, the great Liberal agitator of his times, he calls him in all his letters, "seducer, vase of injuries, scorpion, cruel wolf".

The pacific St. Thomas of Aquinas forgets the calm of his cold syllogisms when he hurls his violent apostrophe against William of St. Amour and his disciples: "Enemies of God" he cries out, "ministers of the devil, members of antichrist, ignorami, perverts, reprobates!" Never did the illustrious Louis Veuillot speak so boldly. The seraphic St. Bonaventure, so full of sweetness, overwhelms his adversary Gerard with such epithets as "impudent, calumniator, spirit of malice, impious, shameless, ignorant, impostor, malefactor, perfidious, ingrate!" Did St. Francis de Sales, so delicately exquisite and tender, ever purr softly over the heretics of his age and country? He pardoned their injuries, heaped benefits on them even to the point of saving the lives of those who sought to take his, but with the enemies of the Faith he preserved neither moderation nor consideration. Asked by a Catholic, who desired to know if it were permissible to speak evil of a heretic who propagated false doctrines, he replied: "Yes, you can, on the condition that you adhere to the exact truth, to what you know of his bad conduct, presenting that which is doubtful as doubtful, according to the degree of doubt which you may have in this regard." In his Introduction to the Devout Life, that precious and popular work, he expresses himself again: "If the declared enemies of God and of the Church ought to be blamed and censured with all possible vigor, charity obliges us to cry wolf when the wolf slips into the midst of the flock and in every way and place we may meet him."

But enough. What the greatest Catholic polemists and Saints have done is assuredly a fair example for even the humblest defenders of the Faith. Modern Ultramontanism has never yet surpassed the vigor of their castigation of heresy and heretics. Charity forbids us to do unto another what we would not reasonably have them do unto ourselves. Mark the adverb reasonably; it includes the entire substance of the question.

The essential difference between ourselves and the Liberals on this subject consists in this, that they look upon the apostles of error as free citizens, simply exercising their full right to think as they please on matters of reli gion. We, on the contrary, see in them the declared enemies of the Faith, which we are obligated to defend. We do not see in their errors simply free opinions, but culpable and formal heresies, as the law of God teaches us they are. By virtue of the assumed freedom of their own opinions, the Liberals are bound not only to tolerate but even to respect ours; for since freedom of opinion is, in their eyes, the most cardinal of virtues, no matter what the opinion be, they are bound to respect it as the expression of man's rational freedom. It is not what is thought, but the mere thinking that constitutes the standard of excellence with them. To acknowledge God or deny Him is equally rational by the standard of Liberalism, and Liberalism is grossly inconsistent with itself when it seeks to combat Catholic truths, in the holding of which there is as much exercise of rational freedom, in the Liberal sense, as in rejecting them. But our Catholic standpoint is absolute; there is but one truth, in which there is no room for opposition or contradiction. To deny that truth is unreasonable; it is to put falsehood on the level with truth. This is the folly and sin of Liberalism. To denounce this sin and folly is a duty and a virtue. With reason, therefore, does a great Catholic historian say to the enemies of Catholicity: "You make yourselves infamous by your actions, and I will endeavor to cover you with that infamy by my writings." In this same way the law of the Twelve Tables of the ancient Romans ordained to the virile generations of early Rome: Adversus bostem aeterna auctoritas esto, which may be rendered: "To the enemy no quarter."

Personal Polemics And Liberalism

"It is all well enough to make war on abstract doctrines" some may say, "but in combating error, be it ever so evident, is it so proper to make an attack upon the persons of those who uphold it?" We reply that very often it is, and not only proper, but at times even indispensable and meritorious before God and men.

The accusation of indulging in personalities is not spared to Catholic apologists, and when Liberals and those tainted with Liberalism have hurled it at our heads, they imagine that we are overwhelmed by the charge. But they deceive themselves. We are not so easily thrust into the background. We have reason - and substantial reason - on our side. In order to combat and discredit false ideas, we must inspire contempt and horror in the hearts of the multitude for those who seek to seduce and debauch them. A disease is inseparable from the persons of the diseased. The cholera threatening a country comes in the persons of the infected. If we wish to exclude it, we must exclude them. Now ideas do not in any case go about in the abstract; they neither spread nor propagate of themselves. Left to themselves - if it be possible to imagine them apart from those who conceive them - they would never produce all the evil from which society suffers. It is only in the concrete that they are effective, when they are the personal product of those who conceive them. They are like the arrows and the balls which would hurt no one if they were not shot from the bow or the gun. It is the archer and the gunner to whom we should give our first attention; save for them, the fire would not be murderous. Any other method of warfare might be Liberal, if you please, but it would not be common sense.

The authors and propagators of heretical doctrines are soldiers with poisoned weapons in their bands. Their arms are the book, the journal, the lecture, their personal influence. Is it sufficient to dodge their blows? Not at all; the first thing necessary is to demolish the combatant himself. When he is hors de combat, he can do no more mischief.

It is therefore perfectly proper not only to discredit any book, journal or discourse of the enemy, but it is also proper, in certain cases, even to discredit his person; for in warfare, beyond question, the principal element is the person engaged, as the gunner is the principal factor in an artillery fight and not the cannon, the powder, and the bomb. It is thus lawful, in certain cases, to expose the infamy of a Liberal opponent, to bring his habits into contempt and to drag his name in the mire. Yes, this is permissible, permissible in prose, in verse, in caricature, in a serious vein or in badinage, by every means and method within reach. The only restriction is not to employ a lie in the service of justice. This never. Under no pretext may we sully the truth, even to the dotting of an "i'" As a French writer says: "Truth is the only charity allowed in history," and, we may add, in the defense of religion and society.

The Fathers of the Church support this thesis. The very titles of their works clearly show that, in their contests with heresy, their first blows were at the heresiarchs. The works of St. Augustine almost always bear the name of the author of the heresy against which they are written: Contra Fortunatum Manichoeum, Adversus Adamanctum, Contra Felicem, Contra Secundinum, Quis fuerit Petiamus, De gestis Pelagii, Quis fuerit julianus, etc. Thus, the greater part of the polemics of this great Father and Doctor of the Church was personal, aggressive, biog raphical, as well as doctrinal - a hand-to-hand struggle with heretics, as well as with heresy. What we here say of St. Augustine we can say of the other Fathers. Whence do the Liberals derive their power to impose upon us the new obligation of fighting error only in the abstract and of lavishing smiles and flattery upon them? We, the Ultramontanes, will fight our battles according to Christian tradition and defend the Faith as it has always been defended in the Church of God. When it strikes, let the sword of the Catholic polemist wound, and when it wounds, wound mortally. This is the only real and efficacious means of waging

A Liberal Objection To Ultramontane Methods

The Liberals tell us that our violent methods of warfare against them are not in conformity with the Pope's counsels to moderation and charity. Has he not exhorted Catholic writers to a love of peace and union, to avoid harsh, agg ressive and personal polemics? How then can we Ultramontanes reconcile the Holy Father's wishes with our fierce methods?

Let us consider the force of the Liberals' objection. To whom does the Holy Father address these repeated admonitions? Always to the Catholic press, to Catholic journalists, to those who are supposed to be worthy of the name. These counsels to moderation and charity, therefore, are always addressed to Catholics, discussing with other Catholics free questions, i.e., those not involving established principles of faith and morality, and they do not in any sense apply to Catholics waging a mortal combat with the declared enemies of the Faith.

There is no doubt that the Pope here makes no allusion to the incessant battles between Catholics and Liberals, for the simple reason that Catholicity is truth and Liberalism heresy, between which there can be no peace, but only war to the death. By consequence, therefore, it is certain that the Pope intends his counsels to apply to our "family quarrels" unhappily much too frequent, and that by no means does he seek to forbid us from waging an unrelenting strife with the eternal enemies of the Church, whose hands, filled with deadly weapons, are ever lifted against the Faith and its defenders.

Therefore, there can be no contradiction between the doctrine we expound and that of the briefs and allocutions of the Holy Father on the subject, provided that logically both apply to the same matter under the same respect, which holds perfectly in this instance. For how can we interpret the words of the Holy Father in any other way? It is a rule of sound exegesis that any passage in Holy Scripture should always be interpreted according to the letter, unless such meaning be in opposition to the context; we can only have recourse to a free or figurative interpretation when this opposition is obvious. This rule applies also to the interpretation of pontifical documents.

How could we suppose the Pope to be in contradiction with all Catholic tradition from Jesus Christ to our own times? Is it for a moment admissible that the style and method of most of the celebrated

Catholic polemists and apologists from St. Paul to St. Francis de Sales should be condemned by a stroke of the pen? Clearly not, for if we were to understand the Pope's counsels to moderation and calm in the sense in which the Liberal conclusion would construe them, we should evidently have to answer, "Yes." Consequently, we must conclude that the Holy Father's words are not addressed to Catholics battling with the enemies of Catholicity, but only to Catholics controverting on free questions amongst themselves.

Common sense itself shows this. Imagine a general in the midst of a raging battle, issuing an order to his soldiers not to injure the enemy too severely! Imagine a captain rushing up and down the ranks shouting to his soldiers, "Be careful! Don't hurt the enemy! Attention there! Don't aim at the heart!"

What more need be said! Pius IX has given us an explanation of the proper meaning of his words. On a memorable occasion he calls the sectaries of the Commune demons; and worse than demons the sectaries of Liberalism. Who then need fear to thunderbolt such an enemy with epithets too harsh and severe?

In vain do the Liberals cite the words of Leo XIII in the encyclical Cum Multa, exhorting Catholics to avoid violence in the discussion of the sacred rights of the Church, and to rely rather upon the weight of reason to gain victory; for the words have reference to polemics between Catholics discussing the best means to preserve their common cause, and by no means apply as a rule to govern polemics with the sectaries of Liberalism. The intrinsic evidence of the encyclical proves this beyond cavil. The Pope concludes by exhorting all associations and individual Catholics to a still closer and more intimate union, and after pointing out the inestimable advantages of such a union, he instances, as the means of preserving it, that moderation of language and charity of which we are speaking. The argument is plain: the Pope recommends moderation and charity to Catholic writers as a means of preserving peace and mutual union. Clearly, this peace and union is between Catholics and not between Catholics and their enemies. Therefore, the moderation and charity recommended by the Pope to Catholic writers applies only to Catholic polemics between Catholics on free questions. Would it not be absurd to imagine that there could be any union between truth and error, therefore between the advocates of truth on the one side and error on the other? Irreconcilable opposites never unite. One or the other must disappear.

The Civilta Cattolica's Charity To Liberals

Charity in controversy with Liberals would be like taking a serpent to ones bosom. It would be as if one embraced some loathsome contagious disease with the foolish notion that to court it would secure immunity from its fearful ravages. Notwithstanding the plain common sense of the situation and the memorable warning of Our Lord that he who loves the fire shall perish in it, some foolish Catholics join with the Liberals in their cry for a magnanimous display of charity on our part when we wage war against them.

Lest our competence to judge in so important a matter be called into question, we will cite as authority on this subject the foremost religious journal of the world, the Civilta Cattolica, founded by Pius IX himself and confided by him to the conduct of the fathers of the Society of Jesus. The Civilta, never suffering an instant of repose to Italian Liberalism, has often been reproached for its want of charity towards the Liberals. Replying to these pharisaical homilies on the measure of charity due them, the Civilta published a delightfully humorous, and at the same time solidly philosophical article, some passages of which we here transcribe for the consolation of our Liberals - and those tainted Catholics who make common cause with them - in decrying Ultramontane methods: "De Maistre said that the Church and the Pope have never asked anything but truth and justice for their cause. On the other hand, the Liberals, no doubt on account of the horror they naturally entertain for truth, and above all, for justice, are always demanding charity.

"For more than a dozen years have we, on our part, been witness to this curious spectacle given us by Italian Liberals. With tears in their eyes, they never cease imploring our charity. Their importunities have at last become insupportable; they have lost all sense of shame; supplicatingly, in the press, in verse, in their brochures, in their journals, in public and private letters - anonymous and pseudonymous - directly or indirectly, they beg us, for the love of God, to show them some charity. They beseech us not to give them over to the ridicule of their neighbors, not to expose to an inspection so detailed, so minute, their sublime writings, not to be so obstinate in subjecting their glorious exploits to such a strong search - light, to close our eyes and our ears to their blunders, their solecisms, their lies, their calumnies, their obscurities, in a word, to let them live in peace.

"The Liberals have imitated, by this edifying conversion to the love of mendicancy, another not less celebrated and not less edifying conversion, that of a rich miser to the virtue of alms-giving. The same miser happening to be present at a sermon which was intended to be a very ardent exhortation to the practice of alms-giving, was so impressed that he imagined himself to be a veritable convert. In truth he was so touched by the sermon that, on going out of the Church, he exclaimed: 'It would be impossible for any good Christian who has heard this discourse henceforth not to give from time to time something in charity.' And so it is with our Liberals. After having shown (according to the measure of their means) by their acts and their writings that they have a love for charity equal to the devil's for holy water, when they hear it spoken of, they suddenly remember that there exists in the world a thing called charity, which might on certain occasions prove very profitable to them. So they show themselves distractedly enamored with it and vociferously demand it from Pope, bishop, clergy, religious, journalists, and everybody, even from the editors of the Civilta. It is curious to follow all the excellent reasons they offer in their own favor!

"To believe them, it is not in their own interest at all that they hold such language! Heavens, no! When they speak thus, it is entirely in the interest of our holy Religion, which they cherish in their heart's core and which suffers so much from our very uncharitable manner of defending it! They even speak in the interest of the reactionaries themselves, and especially (who would believe it!) in the interest of the editors of the Civilta Cattolica!

"'What obliges you to enter into these quarrels?" they confidentially say to us. 'Have you not enough enemies already? Be tolerant and your adversaries will be so with you. What do you gain by following this wretched occupation, like a dog spending his life barking at robbers? If in the end you are beaten, struck down, to whom do you owe it, if not to yourselves and that indomitable animosity of yours, which is ever seeking the lash?' "What sage and disinterested reasoning, whose only defect is that it singularly resembles that which the police officer urged upon Renzo Tramaglino, in the romance The Betrothed, when he essayed to conduct him to prison by persuasion, fearing that if he used force, the young man would offer resistance ... The only result of these exhortations was to confirm Renzo in his design to pursue a course just opposite to that which the officer advised.

"This design, to speak properly, we are strongly tempted also to form, for in truth, we cannot persuade ourselves that the injury, great or small, which we cause religion, matters much or little to the Liberals, nor that they would give themselves so much trouble for our sakes. We are persuaded, on the contrary, that if the Liberals really believed that our manner of acting were hurtful to religion or to ourselves, they would carefully refrain from adverting to it, but rather encourage us in it by their applause. We even conclude that the zeal which they show in our regard and their reiterated prayers to us to modify our style are the surest signs that religion suffers nothing from our methods, and moreover that our writings have some readers, which is always some slight consolation to the writer.

"But as many of them (the Liberals) continue to beg, and as they have recently published a little book at Perugia entitled What Does the Catholic Party Say? - which they devote entirely to a demand upon the Civilta Cattolica for charity - it will be useful, in beginning this fifteenth series of our Review, to confute once more the old objections with the old answers. It will be in fact a great charity, not such indeed as the Liberals beg of us, but one truly very meritorious, the charity of listening to them with patience for the hundredth time."

A Liberal Sophism And The Church's Diplomacy

Liberals often urge as an objection to Ultramontane vigor the fact that the Church herself enters into amicable relations with Liberal governments and personages, or what comes to the same thing, with Liberalism itself.

If the Church can take such a position, surely Ultramontanes, who are looked upon as the vanguard of the Church, may find an example in this her policy worthy of imitation.

We reply. We are to consider these relations as official amities, and nothing more. They by no means suppose any particular affection for the persons who are their object, much less approbation of their actions, and infinitely less any adhesion to their doctrines or the approval of them.

In the first place, we must remember that there are two ministrations in the Church of God: one which we may call apostolic, relative to the propagation of the Faith and the salvation of souls; the other, which we may very properly term diplomatic, having for its subject human relations with the powers of the world.

The first is the most noble; properly speaking, it is the principal and essential ministration. The second is inferior and subordinate to the first, of which it is only the auxiliary. In the first, the Church is intolerant and uncompromising; in this she goes strai ght to her end and breaks rather than bends: frangi non flecti. Witness in this respect the persecutions she has suffered. When it is a question of divine rights and divine duties, neither attenuation nor compromise is possible. In the second ministration, the Church is condescending, benevolent and full of patience. She discusses, she solicits, she negotiates, she praises, that she may soften the hard; she is silent sometimes, that she may better succeed; seems to retreat, that she may better advance and soon attain a better vantage. In this order of relations, her motto might be: flecti non frangi. When it is a question of mere human relations, she comports herself with a certain flexibility and admits the usage of special resources.

In this domain, everything that is not declared bad and prohibited by the law common to the ordinary relations of men is lawful and proper. More explicitly, the Church deems that she may properly make use of all the resources of an honest diplomacy.

Who would dare reproach her for accrediting ambassadors to bad and even infidel governments, and on the other hand, in accepting ambassadors from them; for honoring their noble and distinguished families by her courtesies and enhancing their public festivities by the presence of her legates? "But why," interrupt the Liberals, "should you manifest such detestation for Liberalism and so vehemently combat Liberal governments, when the Pope thus negotiates with them, recognizes them, and even confers distinctions on them?" We can best answer this foolish thrust by a comparison. You, we will suppose, are the father of a family. You have five or six daughters, whom you have brought up in the most scrupulous and rigorous virtue. Opposite to your house, or perhaps next door, we will imagine, dwell some neighbors of blemished reputation. You command your daughters, without cessation, under no circumstances to have ought to do with these people. They obey you strictly. But suppose now that some matter should arise relative to both you and your neighbor's interest in common, such as the paving of a street, the laying of a water main, etc. This obliges you to consult and advise with your neighbors as to this common interest. In your intercourse with them, you treat them with the usual courtesies of society and seek to conclude the business on hand in an harmonious way. Would your daughters, therefore, be justified in declaring that, as you their father had entered into certain relations with these nei ghbors and extended to them the usual courtesies of society, so should they be allowed to associate with them; as long as you their father had thus entered into relation with them, so they had a right to conclude that they were people of good morals?

The Church is the home of good people (or of those who ought to be and desire to be), but she is surrounded by governments more or less perverted, or even entirely perverted. She says to her children: "Detest the maxims of these governments; combat these maxims; their doctrine is error; their laws are iniquitous." At the same time, in questions when her own and sometimes their interests are involved, she finds herself under the necessity of treating with the heads or the representatives of these governments, and in fact she does treat with them, accepts their compliments, and employs in their regard the formula of the polished diplomacy in usage in all countries; she negotiates with them in relation to matters of common interest, seeking to make the best of the situation in the midst of such neighbors. In thus acting does she do anything wrong) By no means. Is it not ridiculous then for a Catholic, availing himself to this example, to hold it up as a sanction of doctrines which the Church has never ceased to condemn, and as the approbation of a line of conduct which she has ever combatted?

Does the Church sanction the Koran when she enters into negotiations, power to power, with the sectaries of the Koran? Does she approve of polygamy because she receives the presents and embassies of the Grand Turk? Well, it is in this way that the Church approves of Liberalism when she decorates its kings or its ministers, when she sends her benedictions, simple formulae of Christian courtesy, which the Pope extends even to Protestants. It is a sophism to pretend that the Church authorizes by such acts what she has always condemned by other acts. Her diplomatic can never frustrate her apostolic ministration, and it is in this latter that we must seek the seeming contradictions of her diplomatic career.

How Catholics Fall Into Liberalism

Various are the ways in which a faithful Christian is drawn into the error of Liberalism.

Very often corruption of heart is a consequence of errors of the intellect, but more frequently still, errors of the intellect follow the corruption of the heart. The history of heresies very clearly shows this fact. Their beginnings nearly always present the same character, either wounded self love or a grievance to be avenged; either it is a woman that makes the heresiarch lose his head and his soul, or it is a bag of gold for which he sells his conscience.

Error nearly always has its origin, not in profound and laborious studies, but in the triple-headed monster which St. John describes and calls Concupiscentia carnis, concupiscentia oculorum, superbia vitae 'Concupiscence of the flesh, concupiscence of the eyes, the pride of life." Here are the sources of all error, here are the roads to Liberalism. Let us dwell on them for a moment.

1. Men become Liberal on account of a natural desire for independence and for an easy life.

Liberalism is necessarily sympathetic with the depraved nature of man, just as Catholicity is essentially opposed to it. Liberalism is emancipation from restraint; Catholicity the curb of the passions. Now, fallen man, by a very natural tendency, loves a system which legitimatizes and sanctifies his pride of intellect and the license of passion. Hence, Tertullian says, "The soul, in its noble aspirations, is naturally Christian." Likewise may it be said that man, by the taint of his origin, is born naturally Liberal. Logically then does he declare himself a Liberal in due form when he discovers that Liberalism offers a protection for his caprices and an excuse for his indulgences.

2. Men become Liberal by the desire for advancement in life. Liberalism is today the dominating idea; it reigns everywhere and especially in the sphere of public life. It is therefore a sure recommendation to public favor.

On starting out in life, the young man looks around upon the various paths that lead to fortune, to fame, to glory, and sees that an almost indispensable condition of reaching the desired goal is, at least in our times, to become Liberal. Not to be Liberal is to place in his way, at the outset, what appears to be an insurmountable obstacle. He must be heroic to resist the Tempter, who shows him, as he did Jesus Christ in the desert, a splendid future, saying : Haec omnia tibi dabo si cadens adoraveris me: "All this will I give thee, if, falling down, thou wilt adore me." Heroes are rare, and it is natural that most young men beginning their career should affiliate with Liberalism. It promises them the assistance of a powerful press, the recommendation of powerful protectors, the potent influence of secret societies, the patronage of distinguished men. The poor Ultramontane requires a thousand times more merit to make himself known and to acquire a name, and youth is ordinarily little scrupulous. Liberalism, moreover, is essentially favorable to that public life which this age so ardently pursues. It holds out as tempting baits public offices, commissions, fat positions, etc., which constitute the organism of the official machine. It seems an absolute condition for political preferment. To meet an ambitious young man who despises and detests the perfidious Corrupter is a marvel of God's grace.

3. Men become Liberal out of avarice, or the love of money. To get along in the world, to succeed in business, is always a standing temptation of Liberalism. It meets the young man at every turn. Around him in a thousand ways does he feel the secret or open hostility of the enemies of his faith. In mercantile life or in the professions he is passed by, overlooked, ignored. Let him relax a little in his faith, Join a forbidden secret society, and lo, the bolts and bars are drawn; he possesses the "open sesame" to success! Then the invidious discrimination against him melts in the fraternal embrace of the enemy, who rewards his perfidy by advancing him in a thousand ways. Such a temptation is difficult for the ambitious to withstand. Be Liberal, admit that there is no great difference between men's creeds, that at the bottom they are really the same after all. Proclaim your breadth of mind by admitting that other religious beliefs are just as good for other people as your faith is for you; they are, as far as they know, just as right as you are; it is largely a question of education and temperament what a man believes; and how quickly you are patted on the back as a "broad-gauged" man who has escaped the narrow limitations of his creed. You will be extensively patronized, for Liberalism is very generous to a convert. "Falling down adore me, and I will give you all these things' " says Satan yet to Jesus Christ in the desert.

Such are the ordinary causes of perversions to Liberalism; from these all others flow. Whoever has any experience of the world and the human heart can easily trace the others.

Permanent Causes Of Liberalism

Liberalism is spread around us like a network. Its web is being constantly spun round about us as spiders weave their meshes for insects. Where one is brushed away, two are multiplied. What is the reason for this?

Philosophy teaches us that the same sources which produce also preserve and increase things. Per quae gignitur, per eadem et servatur et augetur. What then are the permanent causes of Liberalism?

1. Corruption of morals: The theater, literature, public and private morals are all saturated with obscenity and impurity. The result is inevitable; a corrupt generation necessarily begets a revolutionary generation. Liberalism is the program of naturalism. Free thought begets free morals, or immorality - Restraint is thrown off and a free rein given to the passions. Who thinks what he pleases will do what he pleases. Liberalism in the intellectual order is license in the moral order. Disorder in the intellect begets disorder in the heart, and vice-versa. Thus does Liberalism propagate immorality, and immorality Liberalism.

2. Journalism: Incalculable is the influence exercised without ceasing by the numerous publications which Liberalism spreads broadcast. In spite of themselves, by the ubiquity of the press, people are forced to live in a Liberal atmosphere. Commerce, the arts, literature, science, politics, domestic and foreign news, all reach us in some way through Liberal channels and come clothed in a Liberal dress. Unless one is on his guard, he finds himself thinking, speaking and acting as a liberal. Such is the tainted character of the poisoned air we breathe! Poor people, by very reason of their simple good faith, absorb more easily the poison than anyone else; they absorb it in prose, in verse, in pictures, in public, in private, in the city, in the country, everywhere. Liberal doctrines ever pursue them and, like leeches, fasten onto them, never to relax their hold. Its work is rendered much more harmful by the particular condition of the disciple, as we shall see in our third count.

3. General ignorance in matters of religion: In weaving its meshes around the people, Liberalism has applied itself to the task of cutting them off from all communication with that which alone is able to lay bare its imposture - the Church. For the past two hundred years,

Liberalism has striven to paralyze the action of the Church, to render her mute, and - especially in the Old World - to leave her merely an official character, so as to sever her connections with the people. The Liberals themselves have avowed this to be their aim: to destroy the reli gious life, to place every hindrance possible in the way of Catholic teaching, to ridicule the clergy and to deprive them of their presti ge. In Italy and France today, see the thousand and one artificial arrangements thrown around the Church to hinder and hamper her actions, to render ineffectual her opposition to the flood of Liberalism. The concordats, such as are observed at the present time, are so many iron collars which Liberalism has placed around her neck to stifle her. Freemasonry in Europe and South America are constantly seeking to bind her hand and foot, that she may be put at its satanic mercy. By open and secret means, this organization has sought to undermine her discipline in every country where it has obtained a footing. Between her and the people, it seeks to dig a deeper and deeper abyss of hate, prejudice and calumny. Naturalism, the denial of the supernatural, it inculcates everywhere. To divorce the entire life of the people from her influence - by the institution of civil marriage, by civil burial and divorce, by teaching the insidious doctrine that society as such has no religious relations or obligations and that man as a social and civil being is absolutely independent of God and His Church and that religion is a mere private opinion to be entertained or not entertained, as one pleases such is the program, such is the effect, and such, in turn, is the cause of Liberalism. But the most pernicious - because the most successful and lasting - propagator of Liberalism is:

4. Secular education: To gain the child is to secure the man. To educate a generation apart from God and the Church is to feed the fires of Liberalism to repletion. When religion is divorced from the school, Liberalism becomes its paramour. Secularism is naturalism, the denial of the supernatural. When that denial is instilled into the soul of the child, the soil of the supernatural becomes sterilized. Liberalism has realized the terrific power of education and with satanic energy is now striving, the world over, for the possession of the child. (With what success we have only to look around us to realize.) In its effort to slay Christ, it decrees the slaughter of the innocents. "Snatch the soul of the child from the breast of its mother the Church," says Liberalism, "and I

will conquer the world." Here is the real battleground between faith and infidelity. he who is victor here is victor everywhere.

How To Avoid Liberalism

How may Catholics, who are perpetually surrounded by the snares of Liberalism, guard themselves securely against its dangers?

1. By the organization of all good Catholics, be their number great or small: They should become known to each other, meet each other, unite together in every locality - every city, town or village, should have a nucleus of Catholic men of action. Such an organization will attract the undecided, give courage to the hesitating and counteract the influence of hostile or indifferent surroundings. If you number only a dozen men of spirit, no matter. Found societies, especially of young men. Put yourselves in correspondence with older societies in your neighborhood, or even at a distance. Link your associations together association with association - as the Roman legions used to form the military tortoise, by uniting shield with shield over their heads. Thus united, be your number ever so small, lift on high the banner of a sound, pure and uncompromising doctrine, without disguise, without attenuation, yielding not an inch to the enemy. Uncompromising courage is always noble, commands sympathy, and wins over the chivalric. To see a man battered by the floods, yet standing firm as a rock, upright and immovable, is an inspiring sight! Above all, give good example, give good example always. What you preach, do! You will soon see how easily you force people to respect you; when you have gained their admiration, their sympathy will soon follow. Proselytes will be forthcoming. If Catholics only understood what a brilliant secular apostolate they could exercise by being open, straightforward, uncompromising practical Catholics, in word and deed, Liberalism and heresy would die a quick death.

2. Good journals: Choose from among good journals that which is best, the one best adapted to the needs and the intelligence of the people who surround you. Read it; but not content with that, give it to others to read; explain it; comment on it, let it be your basis of operations. Busy yourself in securing subscriptions for it. Encourage the reluctant to take it; make it easy for those to whom it seems troublesome to send in their subscriptions. Place it in the hands of young people who are beginning their careers. Impress on them the necessity of reading it; show them its merits and its value. They will begin by tasting the sauce and will at last eat the fish. This is the way

the advocates of Liberalism and impiety work for their journals; so then ought we to work for ours. A good Catholic journal is a peremptory or imperative necessity in our day. Whatever be its defects or inconveniences, its advantages and its benefits will outweigh them a thousandfold. The Holy Father has said that "a Catholic paper is a perpetual mission in every parish." It is ever an antidote to the false journalism that meets you on every side. In general, do all in your power to further the circulation of Catholic literature, be it in the shape of book, brochure, lecture, sermon or pastoral letter. The weapon of the crusader of our times is the printed word.

3. The Catholic school: With all your power support the Catholic school, in deed and in word, with your whole heart and your whole soul. The Catholic school has become in this age the only secure bridge of the Faith from generation to generation. In our own country, we have been compelled to establish our own schools, unaided and alone. The prejudice and intolerance of Liberalism has refused us common justice. While we protest against the wrong and never cease demanding our right, our clear and peremptory duty is to provide the best possible schools of our own, where our children may be educated in the full and only true sense of the word. Where Catholic schools are needed, build them, build them, build them! Never tire in this absolutely necessary work. Bend every energy to it. Archbishop Hughes said, "Not until I have built my school shall one stone of my Cathedral be laid upon another' " This great prelate fully realized what every Catholic today should take as his motto, "The foundation of the parish church is the schoolhouse '" Be the support of the school a burden, be it built and perpetuated at a great sacrifice, its value is beyond estimation, the burden and the sacrifice are featherweights in comparison to the good that arises from the Catholic school. The spiritual life of a parish without a school is tepid, neither hot nor cold. Let the school be the best possible. Too much time or too much care cannot be given to it, for Catholic education amidst the deluge of Liberalism - which has overwhelmed the world - is the ark of salvation. Speak out fearlessly on this matter of education. Say squarely and frankly that irreligious education leads to the devil. An irreligious school is the school of Satan. Danton, a celebrated French revolutionist, continually cried, "Boldness! More boldness!" But we, for our part, must let our constant cry be, "Frankness! Frankness! Light! Light!" Nothing will more quickly put to

flight the legions of Hell, who seduce only under the shelter of darkness.

How To Distinguish Catholic From Liberal Works

Qui male agit odit lucem -- "Everyone that doth evil hateth the light" (John 3:20) -- said our Divine Lord. Iniquity works in obscurity. It is not difficult to discover an enemy who comes to meet us in the broad daylight, or not to recognize as Liberals those who frankly declare themselves to be such. But this sort of frankness is not ordinary to the Liberal sect. On the contrary, it is usually very clever and cautious in concealing its real meaning in various disguises. We may add that often the eye that ought to discover the imposture is not the clear-sighted eye of a lynx. There should therefore be some easy and popular criterion to distinguish, at every instant, the Catholic cry from the infernal birdcall of Liberalism.

It often happens that some project or enterprise is put on foot, some sort of a work is undertaken, whose bearings Catholics cannot promptly or easily apprehend. It may appear indifferent or even innocent enough, and yet it may have its roots in error and be a mere artifice of the enemy - flying our colors to allure us into an ambuscade. It may speak the language of charity, appealing to us from the tenderest side, and ask us to associate ourselves with it in the name of a common humanity. "Sink all differences of creed and let us fraternize on the broader plane of brotherly love" is often its most insidious appeal. Such instances are arising every day of our lives. "Consult the Church" some may say; "its word is infallible and will dissipate all uncertainty." Very true, but the authority of the Church cannot be consulted at every moment and in every particular case. The Church has wisely laid down certain general principles for our guidance, but it has left to the judgment and prudence of each of us the special application of these principles to the thousand and one concrete cases which we have to face every day. Now a case of this kind presents itself to be determined according to our own judgment and discretion. We are asked to give a contribution to such and such an undertaking, to Join such and such a society, to take part in such and such an enterprise, to subscribe to such and such a journal, and all this may be for God or the devil; or what is worse, it may be evil cloaked in the garb of holy things. How shall we guide ourselves in such a labyrinth?

Here are two very practical rules of ready service to a Catholic who is walking on slippery ground:

1. Observe carefully what class of people are the projectors of the affair. Such is the first rule of prudence and common sense. It is based on that maxim of Our Lord: "A bad tree cannot bring forth good fruit." Liberalism is naturally bound to produce writings, works and deeds impregnated with the spirit of Liberalism, or at least tainted with it. Therefore, we must carefully scrutinize the antecedents of the person or persons who organize or inaugurate the work in question. If they are such that you cannot have entire confidence in their doctrines, be on your guard against their enterprises. Do not disapprove immediately, for it is an axiom of theology that not all the works of infidels are sinful, and this axiom can be applied to the works of Liberals. But be careful not to take them immediately for good; mistrust them, submit them to examination, await their results.

2. Observe the kind of people who praise the work in question. This is an even surer rule than the preceding. There are in the world two perfectly distinct currents: the Catholic current and the Liberal current. The first is reflected for the most part by the Catholic press; the second is reflected by the Liberal press. Is a new book announced? Are the beginnings of a new project published? See if the Liberal current approves, recommends and accounts them its own. If yes, the book and the project are judged: they belong to Liberalism. It is evident that Liberalism has inspired them, distinguishing immediately what is injurious or useful to it, for Liberalism is never such a fool as not to understand what is opposed to it or to be opposed to that which is favorable to it. The sects, religious or infidel, have an instinct, a particular intuition (olfactus mentis), as philosophers say, which reveals to them a priori what is good or what is bad for them. Repudiate, then, whatever Liberals praise or vaunt. It is evident that they have recognized - by its nature or by its origin, or as a means or as an end - something in the object so praised that is favorable to Liberalism. The clairvoyant instinct of the sect cannot deceive them. Certain scruples of charity and the habit of thinking well of our neighbor sometimes blind good people to such an extent as to lead them to attribute good intentions where unhappily they do not exist. This is not the case with falsifiers. They always send their shot right to the center; they never credit good intentions where there are none, or even where there are. They always beat the bass-drum in favor of all that advances in any way their own nefarious propaganda. Discredit,

therefore, what you see your known enemies proclaiming with hallelujahs.

It seems to us that these two rules of common sense, which we can call rules of good Christian sense, suffice - if not to enable us to judge definitively every question - at least to keep us from perpetually stumbling over the roughness of the uneven soil which we daily tread and where the combat is always taking place. The Catholic of the age should always bear in mind that the ground on which he walks is undermined in every direction by secret societies, that it is these who give the keynote to anti-Catholic polemics, that unconsciously and very often these secret societies are served even by those who detest their infernal work. The actual strife is principally underground and against an invisible enemy, who rarely presents himself under his real device. He is to be scented, rather than seen; to be divined by instinct, rather than pointed out with the finger. A good scent and practical sense are more necessary here than subtle reasoning or labored theories.

Liberalism And Journalism

The press has grown so omnipresent nowadays that there is no escape from it. It is therefore important to know exactly how to steer our course amidst the many perils that beset Catholics on this score. How then are we to distinguish between journals that merit or do not merit our confidence? Or rather, what kind of journals ought to inspire us with very little and what with no confidence? In the first place, it is clear that such journals as boast of their Liberalism have no claim to our confidence in matters that Liberalism touches on. These are precisely the enemies against whom we have constantly to be on guard, against whom we have to wage perpetual war. This point then is outside of our present consideration. All those who in our times claim the title of Liberalism, in the specific sense in which we always use the term, become our declared enemies and the enemies of the Church of God.

But there is another class of journals less prompt to unmask and proclaim themselves, who love to live amidst ambiguities in an undefined and indefinite region of compromise. They declare themselves Catholic and aver their detestation and abhorrence of Liberalism, at least if we credit their words. These journals are generally known as Liberal Catholic. This is the class which we should especially mistrust, and we should not permit ourselves to be duped by its pretended piety. When we find journals, Catholic in name and in profession, strongly leaning to the side of compromise and seeking to placate the enemy by concessions, we may rest assured that they are being drawn down the Liberal current, which is always too strong for such weak swimmers. He who places himself in the vortex of a maelstrom is sure in the end to be engulfed in it. The logic of the situation brings the inevitable conclusion.

The Liberal current is easier to follow. It is largely made up of proselytes and readily attracts the self love of the weak. The Catholic current is apparently more difficult; it has fewer partisans and friends and requires us constantly to row against the stream, to stem the tide of perverse ideas and corrupt passions. With the uncertain, the vacillating and the unwary, the Liberal current easily prevails and sweeps them away in its fatal embrace. There is no room, therefore, for confidence in the Liberal Catholic press, especially in cases where it is difficult to form a judgment. Moreover, in such cases, its policy of compromise and conciliation hampers it from forming any decisive or absolute judgment, for the simple reason that its judgment has nothing decisive or radical in it; on the contrary, it is always overweighed with a preponderating inclination towards the expedient. Opportunism is its guiding star.

The truly Catholic press is altogether Catholic, that is to say, it defends Catholic doctrine in all its principles and applications; it opposes all false teaching (known as such) always and entirely, opposite per diametrum ["diametrically opposed"], as St. Ignatius says in that golden book of his exercises. Arrayed with unceasing vi gilance against error, it places itself on the frontier, always face-to-face with the enemy. It never bivouacs with the hostile forces, as the compromising press loves to do. Its opposition is definite and determined; it is not simply opposed to certain undeniable maneuvers of the foe, letting others escape its vigilance, but watches, guards, and resists at every point. It everywhere presents an unbroken front to evil, for evil is evil in everything, even in the good which, by chance, may accompany it.

Let us here make an observation to explain this last phrase, which may appear startling to some, and at the same time explain a difficulty entertained by not a few.

Bad journals (we include doctrinally unsound journals under this head) sometimes contain something good. What are we to think of the good thus imbedded with the bad in them? We must think that the good in them does not prevent them from being bad, if their doctrine or their character is intrinsically bad. In most cases this good is a mere artifice to recommend, or at least disguise, what in itself is essentially bad. Some accidentally good qualities do not take away the bad character of a bad man. An assassin and a thief are not good because they sometimes say a prayer or give alms to a beggar. They are bad in spite of their good works, because the general character of their acts, as well as their habitual tendencies, is bad and if they sometimes do good in order to cloak their malice, they are even worse than before.

On the other hand, it sometimes happens that a good journal falls into such or such an error or into an excess of passion in a good cause and so says something which we cannot altogether approve. Must we for this reason call it bad? Not at all, and for a reverse although analogous reason. With it the evil is only accidental; the good constitutes its substance and is its ordinary condition. One of several sins do not make a man bad - above all, if he repent of them and make amends. That alone is bad which is bad with full knowledge, habitually and persistently. Catholic journalists are not angels; far from it; they too are fragile men and sinners. To wish to condemn them for such or such a failing, for this or that excess, is to entertain a pharisaical or jansenistic opinion of virtue, which is not in accord with sound morality!

To conclude, there are good and bad journals; among the latter are to be ranked those whose doctrine is ambiguous or ill-defined. Those that are bad are not to be accounted good because they happen to slip in something good, and those that are good are not to be accounted bad on account of some accidental failings.

Good Catholics, who judge and act loyally according to these principles, will rarely be deceived.

Can Catholics And Liberals Ever Unite?

A question very pertinent to our times and our surroundings is, Should Catholics combine with the more moderate Liberals for the common end of resisting the advance of the revolutionists or extreme Liberals? With some, this is a golden dream; with others, a perfidious snare by which they seek to paralyze our powers and divide us.

What should we think of these would-be unionists, we who wish above all things the wellbeing of our Holy Religion?

In general, we should think such unions are neither good nor commendable. Liberalism, let its form be as moderated or as wheedling as possible, is by its very essence in direct and radical opposition to Catholicity. Liberals are the born enemies of Catholics, and it is only accidentally that both can have interests that are truly common.

It is possible, however, in very rare cases, that a union on the part of Catholics with a Liberal group against the Radicals may prove useful under given conditions. Where such a union is really opportune, it must be established on the following basis:

1. The bond of union should never be neutrality or the conciliation of interests and principles essentially opposed, such as are the interests and principles of Catholics and Liberals. This neutrality or conciliation has been condemned by the Syllabus of Errors of Pope Pius IX and is, consequently, a false basis. Such a union would be a betrayal, an abandonment of the Catholic camp by those who are bound to defend it. An instance would be to compromise Catholic education with Secularism by banishing religious instruction and influences from the school room. The basis of such conciliation is false, as it necessarily sacrifices Catholic interests and principles. It concedes to Secularism what is essential to the integ rity of Catholic education, viz., the formation of the Catholic character in children, and admits the validity of the principle of neutrality. It can never be said, "Let us abstract from our differences of doctrine, etc." Such a loose abdication of principle can never obtain in the Catholic estimation. It would be the same as to say, "In spite of the radical and essential opposition of principles between us, we can, after all, agree in the practical application of these principles." This is simply an intolerable contradiction.

2. Much less could we accord to the Liberal group, with whom a temporary and accidental alliance is formed, the honor of enrolling

ourselves under its banner. Let each party keep distinct its own proper device, or let the Liberals in question range themselves under our ensign, if they wish to fight with us against a common enemy. We can never assume their emblem under any circumstances. In other words, let them unite themselves to us; we can never unite ourselves to them. Accustomed as they are to a varying and motley ensign, it cannot be difficult for them to accept our colors. For us there can be but one flag - the one emblem of the one, unvarying Faith which we ever profess.

3. We must never consider this alliance constant and normal. It can never be anything else than a fortuitous and transient condition, passing away the moment the immediate exigency of its existence ceases. There can be no constant and normal union, except between homogeneous elements. For people of convictions who are radically opposed, to harmonize for any length of time would require continual acts of heroic virtue on the part of both sides. Now heroism is no ordinary thing, nor is it of daily exercise. Such grave incompatibility would simply expose the undertaking to lamentable failure and would build upon contradictory opinions, whose only accord is accidental. For a transitory act of common defense or attack, such an attempt at a coalition of forces is permissible - and even praiseworthy and extremely useful - provided, however, that we never forget the conditions or rules we have already laid down as governing the exceptional circumstances obtaining in a given case; these rules are an imprescriptible necessity. Outside of these conditions, not only should we hold that such a union with any group, for any enterprise whatever, would be unfavorable to Catholics, we should also hold that it would be actually detrimental. Instead of augmenting our forces, as would be the case in the union of homogeneous elements, it would paralyze and nullify the vigor of those who would be able, if alone, to do something for the defense of the truth. Without doubt, as the proverb runs, "Unhappy the one who walks alone' " But there is another proverb equally true which says, "Better seek solitude than bad company." It was St. Thomas, we believe, who said, Bona est unio sed potior est unitas, "Union is good, but unity is better." If we have to sacrifice true unity for the sake of an artificial and forced union, not only is nothing gained, but much is lost.

Experience has always shown that the result of such unions, outside of the conditions just laid down, is barren. Their result always renders the strife even more bitter and rancorous. There is not a single example of such a coalition which served either to edify or consolidate.

An Illusion Of Liberal Catholics

Amongst the illusions entertained by a certain class of Catholics, there is none more pitiable than the notion that the truth requires a great number of defenders and friends. To these people, numbers seem a synonym for force. They imagine that to multiply heterogeneous quantities is to multiply power.

Now true force, real power, in the physical as in the moral order, consists in intensity, rather than in extension. A greater volume of matter equally intense evidently produces a greater effect, not by reason of the increased volume, but by virtue of the augmented intensities contained in it. It is therefore a rule of sound mechanics to seek to increase the extension and number of forces, but always on the condition that the final result be a real augmentation of their intensities. To be content with an increase without consideration of the value of the increment is not only to accumulate fictitious force, but to expose to paralysis the powers which one does possess by the congestion of an unwieldy mass. The millions of Xerxes' army constituted a force of tremendous extension, but they were of no avail against the vigorous intensity of the Greek three hundred at Thermopylae.

Faith possesses a power of its own, which it communicates to its friends and defenders. It is not they who give the truth power, but truth which charges them with its own vigor. This on the condition that they use that power in its defense.

If the defender, under the pretext of better defending the truth, begins to mutilate it, to minimize it, to attenuate it, then he is no longer defending the truth. He is simply defending his own invention, a mere human creation, more or less beautiful in appearance, but having no relation to truth, which is the daughter of Heaven.

Such is the delusion of which many of our brethren are the unconscious victims, through a detestable contact with Liberalism.

They imagine, with blinded good faith, that they are defending and propagating Catholicity. But by dint of accommodating it to their own narrow views and feeble courage, in order to make it, they say, more acceptable to the enemy whom they wish to overcome, they do not perceive that they are no longer defending Catholicity, but a thing of their own manufacture, which they naively call Catholicity, but which they ought to call by another name. Poor victims of self-deception, who at the beginning of the battle, in order to win over the enemy, wet their own powder and blunt the edge and the point of their swords! They do not stop to reflect that an edgeless and pointless sword is no longer a weapon, but a useless piece of old iron, and that wet powder cannot be fired.

Their journals, their books, their discourses veneered with Catholicity but bereft of its spirit and its life - have no more value in the cause of the Faith than the toy swords and pistols of the nursery.

To an army of this kind, be it ten times as numerous as the multitudinous hosts of Xerxes, a single platoon of well-armed soldiers - knowing what they are defending, against whom they are contending, and with what arms they fight in order to defend the truth - is preferable a thousand times over. This is the kind of soldiers we need. This is the kind who have always and will yet do something more for the glory of His Name. They go into the deadly, imminent breach and never flinch. No compromising, no minimizing with them. They plant their banner on the topmost height and form a solid, invincible phalanx around it that not all the legions of Earth and Hell combined can budge a single inch. They make no alliance, no compromise with a foe whose single aim, disguised or open, is the destruction of the truth. They know that the enemy is by nature implacable and that his flag of truce is but a cunning device of treachery.

Of this we will become more and more convinced, if we consider that an alliance of this kind with a false auxiliary group is not only useless to the good Christian in the midst of the combat, but moreover, it is most of the time an actual embarrassment to him and favorable to the enemy. Catholic associations hampered in their onward march by such an alliance will find themselves so impeded that free action becomes impossible. They will end by having all their energies crushed under a deadly inertia. To bring an enemy into the camp is to betray the citadel. It was not until the Trojans admitted the fatal wooden horse within the city walls that Illium [Troy] fell. This combination of the bad with the good cannot but end in evil results. It brings disorder, confusion, suspicion and uncertainty to distract and divide Catholics, and all this to the benefit of the enemy and to our own disaster.

Against such a course la Civilta Cattolica, in some remarkable articles, has emphatically declared. Without the proper precaution, it says, "associations of this kind (Catholic) run the certain danger, not only of becoming a camp of scandalous discord, but also of wandering away from their true principles, to their own ruin and to the great injury of religion '" And this same review, whose authority is of the greatest possible weight, in regard to the same subject, says, "With a prudent understanding, Catholic associations ought chiefly to take care to exclude from amongst themselves not only those who openly profess the principles of Liberalism, but also those who have deceived themselves into believing that a conciliation between Liberalism and Catholicism is possible, and who are known as Liberal Catholics."

Liberalism And Authority In Particular Cases

How is one to tell on his own authority who or what is Liberal, without having recourse to a definitive decision of the teaching Church? When a good Catholic accuses anyone of Liberalism or attacks and unmasks Liberal sophisms, the accused immediately seeks refuge in a challenge of the accuser's authority: "and pray, who are you to charge me and my journal with Liberalism? who made you a master in Israel to declare who is or who is not a good Catholic? and is it from you that must take out a patent on Catholicity?" Such is the last resort of the tainted Catholic on finding himself pushed to the wall. How then are we to answer this opposition? Is the theology of Liberal Catholics sound upon this point?

That we may accuse any person or writing of Liberalism, is it necessary to have recourse to a special judgment of the Church upon this particular person or this particular writing? By no means. If this Liberal paradox were true, it would furnish Liberals with a very efficacious weapon with which, practically speaking, to annul all the Church's condemnations of Liberalism.

The Church alone possesses supreme doctrinal magistery in fact and in right, Juris et facti; her sovereign authority is personified in the Pope. To him alone belongs the right of pronouncing the final, decisive and solemn sentence. But this does not exclude other judgments less authoritative but very weighty, which cannot be despised and even ought to bind the Christian conscience. of this kind are:

1. Judgments of the Bishops in their respective dioceses.
2. Judgments of pastors in their parishes.
3. Judgments of directors of consciences.
4. Judgments of theologians consulted by the lay faithful.

These judgments are of course not infallible, but they are entitled to great consideration and ought to be binding in proportion to the authority of those who give them, in the gradation we have mentioned. But it is not against judgments of this character that Liberals hurl the peremptory challenge we wish particularly to consider. There is another factor in this matter that is entitled to respect, and that is:

5. The judgment of simple human reason, duly enlightened.

Yes, human reason, to speak after the manner of theologians, has a theological place in matters of religion. Faith dominates reason, which ought to be subordinated to faith in everything. But it is altogether false to pretend that reason can do nothing, that it has no function at all in matters of faith; it is false to pretend that the inferior light, illumined by God in the human understanding, cannot shine at all because it does not shine as powerfully or as clearly as the superior light. Yes, the faithful are permitted and even commanded to give a reason for their faith, to draw out its consequences, to make applications of it, to deduce parallels and analogies from it. zt is thus by use of their reason that the faithful are enabled to suspect and measure the orthodoxy of any new doctrine presented to them, by comparing it with a doctrine already defined. zf it be not in accord, they can combat it as bad, and justly stigmatize as bad the book or journal which sustains it. They cannot of course define it ex cathedra, but they can lawfully hold it as perverse and declare it such, warn others against it, raise the cry of alarm and strike the first blow against it. The faithful layman can do all this, and has done it at all times with the applause of the Church. Nor in so doing does he make himself the pastor of the flock, nor even its humblest attendant; he simply serves it as a watchdog who gives the alarm. Opportet allatrare canes "It behooves watchdogs to bark, very opportunely said a great Spanish Bishop in reference to such occasions.

Is not perchance the part played by human reason so understood by those zealous prelates who on a thousand occasions exhort the faithful to refrain from the reading of bad journals and works, without specially pointing them out? Thus do they show their conviction that reason, this natural criterion, illumined by faith, is sufficient to enable the faithful to apply well-known doctrines to such matters.

Does the Index of Forbidden Books itself give the title of every forbidden book? Do we not find under the rubric of "General Rules of the Index" certain principles according to which good Catholics should guide themselves in forming their judgment upon books not mentioned in the Index, but which each reader is expected to apply at his own discretion? Of what use would be the rule of faith and morals if in every particular case the faithful could not of themselves make the immediate application, or if they were constantly obliged to consult the Pope or the diocesan pastor? just as the general rule of morality is the law in accordance with which each one squares his own conscience (dictamen practicum - "practical judgment") in making particular applications of this general rule (subject to correction if erroneous), so the general rule of faith, which is the infallible authority of the Church, is and ought to be in consonance with every particular judgment formed in making concrete applications - subject, of course, to correction and retraction in the event of mistake in so applying it. It would be rendering the superior rule of faith useless, absurd and impossible to require the supreme authority of the Church to make its special and immediate application in every case and upon every occasion which calls it forth.

This would be a species of brutal and satanic Jansenism, like that of the followers of the unhappy Bishop of Ypres, who exacted, for the reception of the Sacraments, such dispositions as would make it impossible for men to profit by that which was plainly intended and instituted for them by Jesus Christ Himself.

The legal rigorism invoked by the Liberalists in matters pertaining to faith is as absurd as the ascetic rigorism once preached at Port Royal; it would result even more disastrously. If you doubt this, look around you. The greatest rigorists on this point are the most hardened sectaries of the Liberal school. But how explain this apparent contradiction? It is easily explained, if we only reflect that nothing could be more convenient for Liberalism than to put this legal muzzle upon the lips and the pens of their most determined adversaries. It would be in truth a great triumph for them, under the pretext that no one except the Pope and the bishops could speak with the least authority, and thus to impose silence upon the lay champions of the Faith, such as were DeMaistre, Cortes, Veuillot, Ward, Lucas and McMaster, who once bore, and others who now bear, the banner of the Faith so boldly and unflinchingly against its most insidious foes. Liberalism would like to see such crusaders disarmed and would prefer above all to succeed in getting the Church herself to do the disarming.

Liberalism As It Is In This Country

Liberalism, whereas essentially one and the same everywhere, presents various faces in different countries. In its essence, it is the denial of the supernatural in whole or in part, but that denial takes a local coloring from place or circumstances. The traditions, customs, prejudices, and idiosyncrasies of a people reflect it at various angles. It is protean in its presentations throughout the world, and to the casual observer, who falls to probe below the appearances of things, it may not seem to manifest itself at all; whereas, in reality, it exists in its subtlest and therefore most dangerous form.

In America it would scarcely seem to exist at all, so ingrained is it in our social conditions, so natural is it to the prevailing modes of thought, so congenital is it with the dominant religious notions about us - and thus providing so congenial a habitat to the Protestant sects. Indeed it is the very constituent of the pseudo-religious and pseudo-moral atmosphere we daily breathe. We can hope to escape its taint only by copious and frequent draughts of orthodox doctrine, by the strictest intellectual vigilance, fortified by supernatural grace. Its aspect in this country is peculiar and fraught with especial danger to those negligent either in faith or morals. Its chief manifestation in the United States is in the form of what is popularly called non-sectarianism. It is a current fallacy, laid down as a fundamental truth that one religion is as good as another, that everyone has the right to believe what be pleases, that differences in creed are after all but differences in forms of expression, that everyone may select his own creed or sect according to his taste - or even altogether repudiate religious beliefs - and finally, that religion is a thing entirely apart from civic and social life. All this of course is secularism in its various degrees - the denial of the supernatural.

In practice, this principle ingratiates itself into social and civic life, directly or indirectly working out to the prejudice of religion and morality: Civil marriage and divorce, mixed marriages and the consequent degeneration of family life, business standards and morality in general pitched on a low key, a vicious literature, a materialistic journalism catering to lax thinking and lax living, religion publicly mocked, scoffed, denied or held indifferently; all these things are coldly regarded as a matter of course, a necessary expedience, things to be condoned and applauded, all on the ground that they are the fruit of liberty. But the most virulent effect crops out in the prevailing educational theory. Here Liberalism manifests itself in its most direful and fullest effects, for it denies to religion the very sphere where it has the strongest right and the fullest reason to use its widest and most lasting influence, viz., upon the minds of children. Secularism, with the instinct of a foe, has here most positively and triumphantly asserted its claim and, under the disguise of strict impartiality and even patriotism, has banished religion from the schoolroom.

That Catholics should not feel the effects of this relaxing atmosphere is scarcely to be expected.

With the air so strongly impregnated with poison, it would be difficult indeed to keep the blood healthy. In not a few instances, they have fallen victims to the plague, and if not always out-and-out corrupted, they become not a little tainted.

Hence we find amongst, if not a large, at least no small number, an easy disposition to compromise or minimize their faith in points of doctrine or practice. The natural tendency in human nature to escape friction and avoid antagonism is unhappily in most instances a ready factor in the direction of concession.

To apologize, excuse, extenuate, soften, explain away this or that point of faith, practice or discipline easily follows from a habit of thought contracted from perpetual contact with Liberalists, with whom everything takes precedence over faith and supernaturalism. This is especially true where Liberalism eschews aggressive action and with a cunning, either satanic or worldly wise, bases its treacherous tolerance upon a supposed generosity of mind or breadth of view. When the supernatural is vaguely identified with the superstitious, faith with credulity, firmness with fanaticism, the uncompromising with the intolerant, consistency with narrowness, in these adjuncts it requires courage, fortitude and the consolation of the assured possession of truth to resist the insidious pressure of a false public opinion. Unless supernaturally fortified and enlightened, human nature under this moral oppression soon gives way to "human respect."

Such are our Liberal surroundings in this country. We cannot escape them. But we are in duty bound to resist their fatal contagion with all the powers of our soul. If we hope to preserve our faith intact, to keep it pure and bright in our souls, to save ourselves from the malign influence of a deadly heresy which is daily leading thousands to perdition, we must be guarded and vigilant in its presence. Amidst a host of swarming foes, our armor should be without flaw from greave to helmet, our weapons well-tempered, keen, and burnished, not only to ward off the hostile blow, but ready to deal home a telling stroke wherever the enemy's weakness exposes him.

It is because we live in the midst of such perplexities, where the ways are devious and where snares are laid for our every footstep, in order to entrap us unawares, that we require to be on our guard in a twofold way: first, by means of a life lived in the state of grace, second, by means of an enlightened reason, which may shine out over our path as a guide to ourselves and a beacon to others. In a special manner is this a need in our country, where Liberalism pretends to be the champion and guardian of natural reason, laying its snares to entrap the unwary and the ignorant. Not in violence but in a treacherous friendliness on the part of Liberalism does the danger lie. A well-instructed Catholic - who thoroughly comprehends the rational grounds of his faith and understands the character of Liberal tactics under our national conditions - can alone successfully cope with the enemy face-to-face. Ultramontanism is the only conquering legion in this sort of warfare. It is for the vanguard of the army to surprise the enemy at his own ambuscade, to mine against his mine and to expose him before he has burrowed under our own camp. Ultramontanism is Catholicity intact and armed cap-a-pie [from head to foot]. It is Catholicity consistent in all its parts, the logical concatenation of Catholic principles to their fullest conclusions in doctrine and practice. Hence the fierce and unholy opposition with which it is constantly assailed. The foe well knows that to rout the vanguard is to demoralize the entire army; hence their rage and fury against the invincible phalanx which always stands fully armed, sleeplessly vigilant and eternally uncompromising.

In this, above all other countriess, do Catholics need to be Watchful, constant and unshaken in their faith, for the disease of Liberalism is virulently endemic. Its assault is perpetual, its weapons invisible, save to the enlightened eye of a resolute and undaunted faith. In Europe, at least on the Continent, Liberalism is violent, aggressive, openly breathing its hatred and opposition. There the war is open; here it is concealed. There the battlefield is the public arena in civic and political life; here the contest is within the social, business and even domestic circle. There it is declared foe against declared foe; here it is friend against friend, even brother against brother, and all the more dangerous in results because friendly, social or domestic relations endure without injury amidst the struggle and are dangerous to the Catholic because these various ties are so many embarrassments to his free action, so many bonds of affection or interest to enchain him. Therefore must be be all vigilant; therefore should his courage be great, his attitude firm and his stand bold, for whereas his circumstances make him friendly to his foe, he must wage a deadly battle for his faith. His task is doubly difficult; be must conquer an enemy who appears his dearest friend.